Fast Lane To Shangri-La

Fast Lane To Shangri-La

The Story Of A Rugby League Family

Dave Sampson

Vertical Editions

First published in the United Kingdom in 2001 by Vertical Editions, Orchard House, New Road, Millthorpe, Sheffield S18 7WN.

ISBN 1904091008

Cover design and typeset by HBA, York.

Printed and bound by Creative Print and Design (Wales), Ebbw Vale.

Contents

This book is dedicated to my mum and dad in thanks for the many qualities they bestowed on us especially resilience.

Acknowledgments

I'd like to thank my whole family for their support whilst writing this book especially my brothers Malcolm and Brian, my son Dean and my niece and nephews Denise, Lee and Paul.

Additionally I would like to acknowledge the help of the following:

Frank Poskett C.C.M. CH.ENG.I.M.E. FL.I.M.E. for use of excerpts from his book 'A Little Bit About Stanley in Bygone Days'.

Brian Robinson Photography of Wakefield, West Yorkshire for various photographs taken in and around Stanley.

Andrew Box Photography of South Elmsall, West Yorkshire for the match photographs of Dean Sampson.

The unknown author of 'A Miners Story'.

Introduction

Is there such a place you ask yourselves, many believe there is. Some claim to have visited many times, some just the once, or are they just fooling themselves thinking that they have been to Shangri-la? Perhaps it is not a place you physically visit? Maybe it's a state of mind that transports you into a Garden of Eden, hidden from the naked eye amongst inaccessible mountains, or is it high amongst the velvet white clouds, constantly adrift on a soft breeze or could it simply be a day trip or a short journey of your soul into space to a galaxy beyond imagination? Is Shangri-la or the visit to it in whatever form, exclusive to a particular person, regardless of creed or colour or is it just another name for heaven?

I know that Shangri-la incorporates a journey, not always a trek in that sense. It does allow you to visit in more ways than simply opening a door into it and it can and does encompass all, individually and collectively. I also know that it has no rules or god or man made morality but there is a price to pay to visit and if you go and should wish to return, the price will vary. Each visit will enrich you but not necessarily in a monetary sense, one thing is for sure, only you can hold the key for Shangri-la.

This story is not meant to be an egotistical view of life but the truth as it happened, the warmth of a family as it twists and turns on its roller-coaster way through the decades, from earliest memories in the 1950's to the present day. No fibs, no lies, the whole truth, although many events have been omitted, there is so much more to tell. It is of a man who made and lost, succeeded and failed, but never, never gave in. The humour, the heartache, the poignancy and the facts. Often accused of being the ultimate optimist and reluctantly agreeing that this was possibly true but he was also tainted by taking people at face value and being double-crossed or outmanoeuvred, call it what you will. But to still keep coming back and then finally going bankrupt only to accept it as the start of another challenge in a different arena, with success his only goal. I am that man.

'Fast Lane To Shangri-la' is the story of a sporting family from a Yorkshire village, predominantly a mining community. Generation after generation would follow their parents down the mine and should they have daughters, then it was probable that they would court and marry a miner, meaning a constant production line of innately tough and competitive people. Like many other villages throughout the British Isles, this particular village bred many athletes of different sports throughout the ages.

My father, George Frederick Sampson decided his children would not become miners and he would be the last. If his sons did not go down the mine and his daughters married no miners then the production line would be broken forever. Having grown up watching his own father struggle with poor health, he was not put down the mine but went into the building trade but in 1937 after the death at 56 of his father, Fred and with a family of his own to feed, he reluctantly became a miner aged 26. He fathered seven children, four boys and three girls. One boy, Victor, died at birth. His eldest, Connie, married Ken, a bricklayer and they produced Denise who in time would run in the 1976 Montreal Olympics.

The next was Brian, he had seven children, five to his first wife Eileen and two to Christine, his second, a boy and a girl. The boy, Paul, became a champion sprinter before going on to be an international rugby union player, one other son also played rugby but this time amateur rugby league.

The third born was Malcolm. He became a top professional rugby league player. He married Avis and had two children, the eldest, Lee, also played professional rugby league and their daughter Vicky, a proficient equestrian, married Craig, another professional rugby league player.

Next came Irene, she was to marry Philip, an architect, and have two daughters who both became teachers.

Then I came along. I married Mavis, the daughter of a miner and we have three children, Dean, Jonathan and Becky. As well as carving out a successful career of my own in professional rugby league, Dean, my eldest also went on to play for Castleford and became an international player and Jonty played as an amateur.

My youngest sister Maire married, John who played amateur rugby league. They produced three girls, Jane, Kate and Sarah - strange that mum and dad's three girls produced only girls. Maire too was a school running champion until being struck down with asthma at 17, apparently my paternal grandmother used to win the village races every year in her day too.

My son Dean and his wife Lorraine, who is a hockey player, have two children. The eldest Olivia, at nearly eight years is showing great promise as an athlete.

Given our family association and success with sport, I reason there must be a hereditary set of genes that we've been handed down through generations. But ultimately I think the innate toughness gene, both mental and physical, is the gene that developed throughout the mining communities and has been the basis on which to build.

I often ask myself if dad's insistence in breaking the line of miners, for what were purely health reasons will eventually dilute the quality of the production line, I suppose only time will tell but then the conditions in the mines have improved since his day. One of his favourite sayings was, 'Women could work down the pit nowadays,' but then dad died in 1980 and Maggie did the rest. There won't be too many miners direct offspring feeding sport in the future for there aren't too many miners left.

Dad was never an icon in sport, his prowess was on the building sites and down the mine, his integrity and belief in a fair day's work for a fair day's pay stood all his offspring in good stead and has been an inspiration to us all every day of our lives. His memory is my inspiration to write this book and the genes that I inherited will give me the strength and will to rise from the ashes like a Phoenix and to set the record straight and emerge with my family's honour intact. Bloodied and bruised we may be but beaten we are not.

An indication of the miner in these parts is well documented throughout the last 250 years and the low esteem in which they were once held can be gleaned from Thomas Hargreaves comments in the latter part of the 18th century. 'They are loose idle men, not much esteemed and not to be depended upon, they are only common colliers and are employed by the day or the week.'

I wish Mr Hargeaves had been around to spend just one day with my father. Better still if it was dependency he was looking for we could have asked the Aussies to include him in their pack during the final test of 1970 when they lost to the British team, some of which were either miners themselves or sons of miners, he would have found out then, the true meaning of dependability.

Frank Hodges in his write up of 'The Men and His Union' said, 'In 1799 men women and children earned their living in the bowels of the earth. The conditions under which they worked were little short of slavery. Tiny children, too frail and tender to stand the fatigue of walking to the place of work underground, were oft times carried on the backs of their fathers and mothers who, by this means, economised the pitiful faltering energy of the infant during the long hours of work. Accidents were numerous; explosions occurred with great force and frequently.'

Prior to 1814 no widows compensation was paid, there were no inquests, only the offer of stout timber for a coffin by the mine owner.

As well as the genes being passed down from generation to generation then so must the tales of the inhumanity practiced by the upper class, small wonder my father was so militant, it took me a long time to comprehend why. I had been shielded, only ever to listen to dad's stories of hacking by pickaxe on a 15 inch coalface or of being buried to the waist by a roof fall, he was such a story teller it came over as a romantic saga and he was my hero, just like John Wayne. Had I known then what I learned as I grew older I would have cheered and revered the Indian or the Negro, for although oceans apart at that time, our forebears had so much in common.

I recently read an article by Professor Brian Sykes and his newly published 'The Seven Daughters of Eve.' His genetic research is a monumental scientific breakthrough. He proves conclusively that from remains found to be thousands of years old, amongst other things one in every hundred white Britons carry DNA from African or Asian decent. Such revelations show that long migration and consequential mixing of races have always been a feature of humanity making talk about racial purity meaningless. As for the origin of the miner in our particular area, I do not believe as some might, that he is a descendant of an original settlement family from Prehistoric, Neolithic or Viking times. Surely the first inhabitants would have been hunter-gatherers and so on to farmers and subsequent trades.

My own family name, Sampson, is of French origin, the historic upheavals of society, the Reformation and migratory consequences indicate that we in all probability, or at least our ancestors, worked in the tin mines of Cornwall and then migrated northwards to seek work, for only people desperate for work or with mining experience would be the original mining families.

Those unfortunates who literally fell into the poverty trap and the way of life that began so long ago and continued for generation after generation, produced a conveyor belt of characters. Hard, uncompromising and competitive, then suddenly finding a game that suited their qualities, they began to live for that magic moment of the kick off on Saturday afternoon only to find that they would be penalised because of their prowess as the mental and physical tough-ness of the northern teams dominated the Northern Union.

It has been well documented elsewhere over last 120 years, the consequences of the birth of Rugby League and the hypocrisy and bigotry of the Rugby Football Union. However progress has been made through the sons and grandsons of miners who are now infiltrating the previously so called academic elite. They are now sharing college and university classrooms and the war mongers are in the minority, supercilious editors of some of the national tabloids and their sports editor cohorts disgracefully hanging on to outmoded ideals, shouting from their headquarters, 'We have won the war.' What war? The war has been over for sometime and did they not learn that in a war there are only casualties to be counted. We of mining and other tough industrial stock are not at war, we are at peace, it will take a long time to heal the wounds created, but we do not fear the Japanese snipers alone on their Fleet Street desert island refusing to accept the outcome and ignoring the ridicule that they bring on themselves.

What the future holds for two games as distinctively dissimilar as they are similar is quite clear, players of the future will change codes, some will play both, some will play one or the other but both codes will remain independent because of their inherent structure and the academic structure of this country and others. In Australia, a reputedly classless society, the two codes coexist and they are World Champions because of their common goal. We can and will emulate them.

As long as we remember my father, George Frederick Sampson's advice that a man has the right to spend his £1 in the pub of his choice and just be grateful if its yours. A very profound statement translated into simpler terms, a man of the future will choose a newspaper for it's unbiased reporting of all aspects of life, not for which political leaning it holds. For those who use their pens in this manner have obviously never known anything more competitive than perhaps out drinking their fellow poison penman.

1. The Sunshine Years

I played and coached Rugby League for a grand total of 34 years before calling it a day in 1994. Wakefield Trinity juniors 1960 to 63, professional player from 1963 to 81, amateur player from 1981 to 84 coupled with grass roots coaching 1978 to 84. I then coached under Mal Reilly at Castleford 1984 to 88. Aged 44, I decided to give myself one more season in the amateur game, 28 games in that year, every one a special event in my calendar. I then coached at Doncaster for two and a half years followed by a brief but enjoyable spell at Nottingham before finishing my career back at Stanley Rangers as coach. I was now 50 and decided it was time to stand back from the game and take a rest. I had lived and breathed rugby since leaving school at 15, I had been fortunate to play with and against the best. I have seen the introduction of substitutes, rule changes galore, four tackles, six tackles, the changes in administration from Bill Fallowfield, David Oxley and Maurice Lindsay through to the present Super League, keeping in touch with the game through my son Dean and acting as agent for my elder brother Brian's son Paul in top flight Rugby Union. This has enabled me to form an advised opinion of the breakdown of the 100-year-old walls of heartache, it is with this pedigree that I feel I can write this book and air my views on all these topics and what the future holds for both sports.

I have endured 22 broken bones, played over 500 games and combined all this with being a publican from the age of 27 and at one time director of a building company to boot. Even through the tough times, I have always remained philosophical, making sure that neither bitterness nor bigotry ever entered my personal domain. I've learned humbleness and its virtues. I've used showmanship and character when I felt it would give positive rewards. I have made mistakes, only now have I learned to live with them and turn the tide.

Only someone who has packed into life what I did, the sheer volume, can have any idea what life can be like in the fast lane, on a seemingly endless journey. This book is about exactly that. I hope people will be wiser for reading it and accept what life can throw at you, but appreciate that life is for sharing and caring with the knowledge and satisfaction that you did what you thought was right at the time and you gave it your best shot and always. If on your journey through life you stopped off in Shangri-la, deem yourself fortunate. I do.

I was born on August 6th, 1944. I don't recall it myself but apparently on my first birthday Enola Gay dropped its payload on Hiroshima. I didn't realise until many years later the significance of this but ever since, no matter which birthday I have celebrated, I have always spared a thought for the unfortunates of this event.

The Second World War was for a long time insignificant because even on reaching my teens in school, my history lessons had progressed, or was it stuttered, as far as Richard III (my last four months at Stanley Secondary Modern were spent erecting the new cricket nets and posts behind the Wheatsheaf pub). Although academically I was always in the top few of my mixed year, I knew very little of modern history. My education was restricted to seeing Audie Murphy as 'Billy the Kid' or Richard Widmark in 'To the Halls of Montezuma' at the local picture house. I know this gave a slant to my way of addressing life but it was hardly my fault. School was never something I relished, in fact on my first day at Bottomboat C of E, I was back at home hiding behind the washer before mum got back. When she found me I was duly returned to class.

These school days are vague to me but not the out of school times or holidays. Very little time was spent indoors, dad was in bed when on night shift, mum was either washing, baking or cooking, so we were under her feet. 'Go out and play' she would tell us. Sometimes our Malc would take me to uncle Frank's farm to help with the harvesting or auntie Ivy would let me help with the pigs. I remember one occasion when the cows were being milked and I was stood behind the cow, my uncle informed me, 'Ah David, don't stand at back of cows son or tha'll regret it.' But I knew everything and paid no attention, I carried on watching, the bucket was half-full with milk, the cow kept coughing, I was fascinated at my uncle squeezing the milk teats. Suddenly the cow started to discharge its dung-clap, call it what you will, I stepped back instead of sideways, the cow coughed, the dung sprayed and covered me from head to toe. I ran from the farmyard in total panic, I can still remember everyone rolling about with laughter and uncle Frank's words will stay with me forever, 'Ah David, don't ever say I didn't warn thee.' I was then hosed down with cold water, clothes and all, then sent home. I ran all the way.

Other summer days we would play cricket, soccer, rugby, marbles, cowboys and Indians, we would make our own bows and arrows and soon learned which trees to use for bows and which for arrows, knowledge handed down over the years I suppose, just as Geronimo or Cochise had.

It was on one such occasion that we were playing behind the shop on the Moorhouse Estate, it was the only shop and still is to this day, on the Moorhouse nothing's changed very much. I still remember it vividly, I was only six and my mate was Vallan Bradbrook, his dad and mine were mates, worked at the same pit. It was all so innocent, I was firing arrows Vallen was kicking a football. He kicked it over the wall that runs at right angles to the shop, he ran and climbed the wall, I heard a screech of brakes and followed him over the wall. Vallen was motionless, his dad and mine had been walking down the hill from their shift at the pit, I can still see them running. Dad sent me to get mum and someone else to get Mrs Bradbrook. That was the first time I'd ever seen my dad shed a tear, Mr Bradbrook was cradling Vallen but he never again saw the light of those balmy summer days. We didn't get the chance to grow up together but I still remember, as I do some of the other tragedies that befell our estate.

The Moorhouse had been built in the late 20's and early 30's, my dad had worked on it as a labourer for Alf Hanks & Son, a local builder. It was significant that in 1955 our Malc went to work as an apprentice bricklayer for Alf Hanks Junior, who had been an apprentice when my dad had worked for his. Malc told me that when he'd got the job young Alf had said to him 'If you're half the man your dad is then you'll do for me lad,' apparently dad was a bit special, but he had insisted that Malcolm was to have an apprenticeship 'I'll not have a lad of mine as a labourer' he had told Alf. Dad had worked as a labourer from leaving school until 1936, when with two children, the money to be earned at the pit was significantly more. Most other families worked in the pits or in work related to its output, Mr Croxall in the signal box on the railway line that took the coal away, he and his family lived at Number 21 we lived at Number 1, exactly 100 yards apart gate to gate. This was our Olympic 100 track.

Ninety five percent of people who lived on the estate, approximately 180 families, knew each other well from either working together, through their children being pals, the local pub or even through being related. The Hargreaves on Moorhouse Grove were cousins of the Hargreaves on Moorhouse Avenue and related to the Fields who likewise lived on the Grove and on the Crescent. The Lockwood's, the Ward's, the Westerman's, who's mother's sister or father's brother married so-and-so, it was endless. New houses with inside toilets, a home on the Moorhouse was usually obtained through a council waiting list and much in demand. I often wonder how our Connie and Ken obtained a house for themselves with a back garden adjoining ours, I felt that dad might have had something to do with it, he was a mate of Harold Colley who was a mate of a councillor, not what you know but who you know I suspect.

Everybody knew everybody, houses were always an open door, bread (home made) left on window ledges, no burglaries, no thefts. The estate had a camaraderie that could never be emulated today, good times and bad were shared together, grief and ill luck were never far away from any family, hazards were just around the corner. The Sandies and the Pastures with the infamous Blue Lagoon, an old open cast mining site surrounded by beautiful farmland, families would spend many happy hours picnicking there.

On one fateful summer evening, the word came onto the estate that two lads had drowned in the Blue Lagoon. People were gathering at their gates and in front of the shop, I had heard early and immediately set off to get there as soon as possible. It was about a mile away but to get to the centre of the lagoon where the platform was that everyone used for diving and swimming was a bit precarious, steep sloping shale banks dropping straight into the T-shaped lagoon, it was cold and deep and dangerous.

I was a non-swimmer at that time so I'd never been in, only swimmers were allowed to go in that was the rule, the older lads were to look after the younger ones, that's how it was. I was negotiating the shale bank when I suddenly began to slide, there was nothing to hold on to,

I was about 30 feet from the water and I knew I was going in, I clawed with both hands but to no avail, down I slid, it seemed to take an age. I could see Albert Louis about 10 yards in front swimming and that he had realised I was in trouble, we met just as I hit the water, I didn't even go under, he swam back to the platform with me in tow, heaved me out and told me in no uncertain terms to go home. It seemed strange, people were stood in silence, a group of three or four were on their knees, I saw a pair of legs sticking out, they were trying to resuscitate one of the boys, alas, it was to be in vain. Roy and Terry Hargreaves drowned. Apparently one could swim the other could not and he had gone to help his brother who was in trouble. They both paid the ultimate price, as did Vallan Bradbrook's elder brother but not swimming, he had been climbing the conker tree not 50 yards from our house, lost his hold and fell to his death, that was in 1941.

Few families escaped some kind of bereavement and it touched everyone, the constant historical intermarriage of families meant that everyone felt the losses in the same way. One could also say that the scales can be balanced by the positives of intermarriage, the wedding celebrations, children and the christening celebrations and so on. We as a family were lucky I suppose but then again, mum told me of my other brother who died at birth that I would have grown up with, so I suppose I needn't have felt guilty, if that's what it was. I'm not sure, maybe mine was yet to come, only time would tell.

My education started at Bottomboat C of E from the age of five until seven. After the first few days we were allowed to make our own way, there were no roads to cross and one parent could easily look after the whole posse. There was also a short cut along the old wagon road and through the bottom end of the Moorhouse but I, like others was reluctant to use it. The bottom end of Moorhouse was very different to the top, families always seemed a bit rougher, they would hang frogs from the clothesline and fire catapults at them. When we had chubbed for logs and brush for our bonfire they would raid our garden after we had gone to bed and steal it, I don't ever remember raiding theirs.

After Bottomboat, we went to Stanley St. Peters C of E from seven to eleven years, nothing significant happened here. I was very slight and quite small, dad would call me 'Belsen Babe' but I could still eat for England, I assume because we were so active we simply burnt it off, as most of us were the same. A fish cake from Beale's fish shop with half a loaf of sliced bread was a banquet in those days, although school meals and milk time sustained us and provided protein.

I failed my 11 plus, the controversial method of designating which school you moved onto. To pass meant Rothwell Grammar, to fail meant 300 yards down the road to Stanley Secondary Modern, they were worlds apart and fierce competitors. There weren't many on Moorhouse that went to Rothwell which I suppose was indicative of the academic prowess of working class families, my dad was the first male Sampson ever to be capable of writing his own name, all his forebears simply made their mark, this is born out on the marriage and birth certificates I have obtained. I suppose he was quite chuffed when on attending my first day at Stanley Modern I was placed in 1A, the 'A' stream usually indicated you were not too far behind those who passed their 11 plus exam. I have often reflected, had I passed, I would have been guided into rugby union and my life would probably have taken a different path altogether.

I knuckled down a bit and thoroughly enjoyed my early years, making new friends. I became a talented chess player and did exceptionally well in subjects such as Art, Drama, English, Geography, History and Religious Knowledge but struggled with others, Maths, Music, Science and Metalwork. In sport I was on the fringe, not quite making either the rugby or football teams unless someone was injured, however, I found I had a gift for cross country running.

The reason I excelled in Religious Knowledge was that I had a distinct advantage over most, dad had made all of us attend Sunday School at the Zion Chapel on Aberford Road, 10 till 12 and 2 till 4 every Sunday from the age of four up until being 13. I believe that the reason he was so strict in making us attend was in the hope that we would emerge wiser, or was it to give him and mum a little peace. Others from the village chose church I don't know to this day why it was the Zion for us.

I left Sunday School under a cloud, it was one Sunday afternoon and Miss Humphries, the teacher always finished with a question and answer session after reading the lesson, if you got it right you could go, a process of elimination.

'David,' Miss Humphries turned to me, she was a tall stern spinster always dressed in dark grey and very serious natured, 'What were the words uttered by Daniel when he emerged from the lion's den?'

'Christ' I thought, that's easy. 'Out of the strong came forth sweetness Miss.'

She was clearly taken aback but quickly regained her composure. 'And kindly tell the class from which book it relates.'

I was quick to fire back, 'That's two questions, why can't I go? I answered the question miss.'

'Don't be insolent and do as I ask Sampson.'

'Oh' I thought, 'It's Sampson now is it?' I don't really know why I behaved in such a rebellious manner but I went on to say, 'I didn't get it from the book miss, I got it from a tin, a Tate & Lyle treacle tin to be exact an' I answered the question so I'm off!'

With that I made my way out, her voice followed me, trembling with rage. 'I'll tell your father! Come back here! Come back! Do you hear?'

I found out later that she'd sent the whole class home, I was a hero to them. One thing I knew for certain though was that she would tell my dad, he walked past her house daily, twice. He would walk past to catch the bus to the club and then again on the way back. I decided to tell mum, I did this as soon as I got home, I wasn't upset and told it as it was, she then broke the news to dad.

'Maybe ah David's growing aht of Sunday School George,' she reasoned, 'None of his mates go.'

'Leave it to me Leah, ahl call an' see woman.'

Mum later told me that sure enough Miss Humphries had collared dad at the bottom of the Bull Wagon Road and told him that I must go and apologise in front of the congregation the following Sunday or I would no longer be welcome. Apparently, dad had ascertained that other children were allowed home when they had answered a question, that was the rule. He had questioned Miss Humphries as to how could he explain that it was different for me, according to mum, Miss Humphries had stated that she didn't have to explain to a 13 year old disrespectful upstart.

Dad relayed the message to mum. 'Tell ah David that if he goes and apologises to the congregation next Sunday it'll all be forgiven, but his dad doesn't think they'll iver forget. It's his decision, I'll say nowt no more about it.'

He never did, nor did I, nor did I ever attend Sunday School again but whenever I see a tin of Tate & Lyle treacle it reminds me of another lesson learned on life's highway and there were many. Dad was a bit of a philosopher, 'A black eye or a bloodied nose all adds character.' he would profess. The ability to express oneself in song was also something he would advocate working on from an early age.

Now I don't think my parents were ever knowingly cruel to us, in fact I know they weren't. But in this day and age some do-gooders might think some of their actions were questionable but I look back and know how proud they were of all of us, just their way of showing it may seem strange by today's way of thinking. Take for instance when I was between the ages of say nine and 12, dad would occasionally bring friends home and after a few beers would say, 'Leah, ask our David to come down and give us a song will you love.'

Mam would come upstairs, shake me and say, 'Ah David, come down an' sing for your dad.'

Now the times varied but it was usually around 12.30 or 1 am, sometimes I didn't want to but I always did. When I came downstairs I would look around the room, it was full of smiling faces, 'He's here' someone would say, 'Turns arrived, nice outfit.'

I was wearing either green and white or blue and white striped pyjamas. I was shy and would make straight for the kitchen, I was too timid to face them and sing, but on my own in the kitchen on my own I was Mario, mum would return to the lounge, I would take a deep breath and begin. 'I'll walk with God, from this day on, I'll talk with God.' From this I would move into 'Because you're mine, the brightest star I see looks down, my love, and envies me.'

Always Mario Lanza songs, I knew them all, all the way through, everyone was happy, I was sent back to bed with a handful of coins. Next morning dad would say, 'Ah David did us proud last night

Leah' and mum would reply, 'We shouldn't wake im in middle of the night George.' and dad would answer, 'Nah Leah, it's character building, stand him in good stead it will when time comes.'

He taught us so much, not that mother didn't make a contribution, God forbid, her family's genes subscribed to make us what we were and she taught us to be equally proud. I vividly recall her support when I would sing in the bath with a mischievously opened window and big Sid Smith would shout across the gardens with his unmistakable stutter, 'G-G-George, can you make that lad of yours sh-sh-shut window, Rose is baking today and she fears c-c-cakes won't rise.'

Dad would be sat on the back steps, stripped to the waist bar a singlet, 'Leah, ask ah David to shut bathroom window will you?'

Mum would come upstairs 'Ah David sing Edelweiss for your mum, and then Michael Row the Boat for Big Sid will you?'

Mum's sense of humour was as subtle as she was gentle. She was a Limer, her father was known as Sweeny Todd the local barber, her mother, a Griffiths was of travelling show stock. I can remember as a child mum's aunts and uncles would park their wagons and caravans on the main road at the front of the Moorhouse stretching 200 yards, then they would scale the wall and enter Gran's back garden for tea and scones before continuing their journey to Heath Common fair. Unfortunately fairs are few these days and we lost touch when Gran and Uncle John died.

Dad's leisure time was sparse so we learned to treasure every moment, his voice only had to suggest a walk, an excursion and we hung on to every word.

'Leah!' I heard my father's voice. 'Ask ah David if he wants to come to Odsal this afternoon to big match.'

It was 1954 I was almost 10 years old, the cup final replay, I thought, 'Yes, not half.'

Mum came in the kitchen, 'Ah David did you hear what your dad asked?'

'Course ah did mam, yes, I'll go get ready.' I never did know why dad could never ask me himself but that's how it always was as kids, 'Leah ask this,' or 'Leah tell so and so,' it was his way, even when you were only feet away from him. I remember he'd say, 'Leah, tell ah David if he keeps picking his nose he'll get his finger stuck.' Mum would reply, 'Ah David stop picking your nose,' it was their fashion. With six of us, all varying ages, from lounge to kitchen to garden to bedroom everyone spoke to each other through mum.

'Mam tell our Irene to hurry up in't bathroom.'

'Mam ah David's stuck is finger in buns.'

'George, are you going to have a word with these two girls about answering back?'

'Stop answering your mother back you two,' would be the reply and sometimes the classic 'If I 'av t' tak this belt off t' ya, ya'll knaw 'bout it.' Dad never did take his belt off, if he had his pants would have been round his ankles, he didn't need to, the shaving belt behind the kitchen door could simply be unhooked, dad could make a cracking noise with this belt that would have scared Lash Laroo.

I had washed, got ready and was waiting for dad when mum insisted that I wear my new gabardine raincoat. 'But mam it's too big, I'm all right as I am.' She proceeded to force me into this coat which made two of me, 'Mam it's a mile too big.'

'You'll grow into it, it's very smart.'

Only the tips of my fingers showed at the end of the sleeves and it was only about six inches from the floor, I was horrified, 'I can't go in this, look at me' I cried, 'I'm not going.'

'Yes you are.' came the reply, 'And you're going in that coat do you hear?'

Well of course I heard I was only about two feet away. With this I stormed out, mum followed me. I made for the dog kennel, mum made for the sweeping brush. The dog came out of the kennel as I went in, I sat at the back and the dog came back in and sat in front of me. Then the brush came in and the dog went for the brush, there was dust and dog hair everywhere, mum was pulling and shoving the brush at me, 'Come out!' she was shouting. The dog was tearing lumps out of the brush, I was coughing with the dust when mum suddenly went quiet, it was then that dad's face appeared at the kennel entrance, he looked in and then vanished. Rex the dog had gone quiet as soon as dad's face appeared, then I heard dad say, 'Leah, tell ah David if he doesn't come aht in two seconds I'll nail door to kennel up while tomorrow.'

'Am coming! Am coming!' I shouted in a panic, slithered out and stood up, head bowed.

'Leah bus'll be here in a minute, I'll walk on, I think he needs a clean up, if he makes it he makes it, if he doesn't he doesn't.'

Mum took me back into the kitchen, soaked a dishcloth and proceeded to wash me down, gabardine raincoat and all. The kitchen floor was covered in dog hairs and so was I.

'Right, get yerself off,' she instructed.

As I reached the gate I looked over to my right, sure enough the bus was coming down Normanton's Hill, 'I'll miss it' I thought. I fair scorched up the Moorhouse Avenue, turned up the snicket and just made it. People were laughing, dad had told them everything, but I was on my way. I sat next to dad, waiting for him to speak.

'Nah then ah David, next time ah want thi to learn to humour thi mother, wear t' coat till tha gets aht sight, then tak it off and sling it over thi arm, then before tha gets home, put it back on. When tha gets home she's happy, tha's happy. An don't forget to say tha's sorry, does tha hear?'

'Yes dad, sorry.'

'Not to me, thi mother, silly lad!'

It took another bus journey from Wakefield to Bradford and I distinctly remember being handed down over everyone's heads and onto the pitch, I have never seen so many people at a match to this day. It was the cup final replay, Halifax versus Warrington, my recollection of the actual match is vague because of the spectacle and excitement. It was late when I arrived home but mum told me in later years that I apologised as I went to bed. I never forgot the lesson I learned that day and mum never needed to scold me too many times after that but I remember once being in the kitchen when mum noticed there were two butterfly buns missing.

'Who's bin in bun tin?' she screamed.

'Not me.' came the chorus of voices.

'I haven't mam honest.' I cried as her glare landed on me.

'What have I told you ah David, not to go in that bun tin,' WHACK! 'Unless I,' WHACK! 'Give you,' WHACK! (By this time I was huddled in the corner) 'Permission.' WHACK!

'Don't it im anymore mam, I ate em.' came our Malc's voice.

'Well you should know better at your age Malcolm.' NO WHACK!

'Aren't you going to whack him mam, eh mam, aren't you going to whack him, you did me?'

'Shut up ah David or a'll send you to bed.' was my answer.

Now my mum might seem a tyrant to some but she wasn't, she was a love, a gentle caring woman who had to make ends meet and if she could have she would have let me down the whole tin.

Some people reading this now and others at the time might simply dismiss us as mischievous children, war babies brought up in what was defined as a development time and prosperous progressive lifestyles that had followed the end of the hostilities were gradual rather than instantaneous. We were mischievous that's a fact but a raid say on Mr Watson's orchard was meticulously planned, the look-outs, timing, rendezvous to share the booty.

On one such occasion Dave Croxall was the lookout, Trev Munn, Colin Westerman and myself were to loot the apple and pear trees exposed in the middle of the cabbage field. We knew we had to work quickly then slip back into the wood and melt into the dense bushes. Here we would make a 'mellow nest' a hole quickly scratched into soft soil, lined with rhubarb leaves to form a base, there we would place our share of the spoils before covering them with more leaves, then soil and a couple of grass sods for camouflage. However, on this particular day as we were stuffing our jumpers with apples and pears (the trick was to tuck your jumper inside your trousers then refasten your snake clasp belt, put the goods down your jumper and within minutes you looked like the Michelin Man) Dave Croxall alerted us that Mr Watson was coming. We dropped from the trees and lay as flat as we could in the cabbages, alas to no avail. He pulled up in his horse and cart, climbed the fence and approached us.

Suddenly Trevor stood up. 'It's no good lads, we're Copt.' he blurted, hands raised above his head.

'Like fuck we are,' I whispered to Colin, 'You run top way, I'll go bottom and meet you behind black railings. Ready? Go!'

We split and ran for our lives all the way around the estate perimeter with Mr Watson's words ringing in our ears. 'I'll get you buggers later, you see.'

Dave had done a runner, so had Colin and myself. Bunny, Trev's nick-name, was taken home where his mum made him tell Watson who was with him, then the hunt began. Dad was out cracking the shaving belt, Mrs Westerman was shouting for Colin. Colin and I made two mellow nests, enjoyed a feast and then made our separate ways home in silence, on our bellies down the wooded planting that fronted the estate. Dad was outside Walt Howe's shop, mum close by. I wasn't giving up until dad had cooled off, I knew I'd get the belt for getting caught but he was due on nights shortly. He'd be in bed when I went to school in the morning so he would have calmed by the next time we met. Mum would have fed him apple pie and custard and I'd only be scolded. Mum came shouting an hour later, I emerged from the grass only a few feet away, she shook her head.

'Have you been there all this time?'

'Yes mum.'

She handed me a carrier bag, 'It'll be dark soon, your dad's gone t' pit, don't be late in.'

The next day we all met up and compared notes. Bunny had been given a 6 o'clock curfew. Dave was too quick, he got off scot-free. Colin got belted. I told them that dad had hit me unmercifully with the shaving belt. We went back to share what was left in the mellow nests. To our dismay in our haste the previous night we had neglect-ed to cover the base with enough rhubarb leaves, the worms and mag-gots were having a party. I blamed Col, he blamed me and Bunny chastised us both, we fired back that he was a grammar school gorby. Dave Croxall suggested that we have a game of cricket. That was how it was. Sam Hargreaves joined us. 'I'm Len Hutton, it's my bat, so I go in first.'

Poor old Mr Watson he always seemed to draw the short straw, this time the woods as we new it, adjoining the Moorhouse had been visited by a timber company. Several men, cabins, tools and saws invaded. This was an exciting event, large tree's came crashing to the ground in abundance, off cuts were available to all who could collect, although it was August a little early for bonfire chumping we had to take advantage of this heaven sent bonanza. It was to be the greatest night of bonfires the Moorhouse had ever seen, occasionally Bottomboaters would show their faces but the logs were substantial and too heavy to transport so far. However we had a hidden weapon, by pure chance one of the loggers axe's had been left in the long grass, over a metre long with a massive steel head honed to split a strand of wick grass.

This axe somehow found its way into our coal store and one evening when I had finished work I took the dog out. A couple of lads were hacking at a tree, a quite substantial tree. I was 15 they about 11, Neil and Nigel had been hacking away for hours with a small hand axe.

'Give us a hand David,' they pleaded.

'Not with that toothpick,' I quipped, 'I'll be back in a second.'

I ran the 60 yards home and was back in a tiff.

'What the bleedin hell is that?'

'Stand back!' I barked and began wielding the axe as if I were a Viking warrior out to impress.

I soon tired but the damage was done, a rest a few more finely aimed whacks and those magic words 'TIMBER' it would fall towards the estate but well short of the garage's I reasoned.

Suddenly a creak, a crack and a groan of timber tearing itself apart.

'Oh Fuck.' shouts Nigel, 'It's tumbling wrong way.'

'Everybody this side I yelled,' the tree seemed to take an age it hit the surrounding shrubs and bushes with a resounding thud, 'Shit' I thought to myself, 'We are in for it now.'

The tree had fallen at a right angle to Mr Watson's driveway, the drive was about eight feet across, shale based and he used it daily for his horse and cart.

'Nobody naw if Watson's home yet?' I asked, heads began shaking.

Neil was first. 'We've been here two hours he ant cum back.'

Followed by Nigel. 'He fucking has he's just pulled onto drive.'

Sure enough another 60 yards around the bend and he would be confronted by this enormous obstacle. I decided to face the music, I began to chop at the tree to one edge of the track, as he emerged around the corner and espied me all alone hacking feverishly at this monster, his face went crimson his cheeks filled with air, a look of shock and exasperation. All in one whoa he steadied the old mare, yanked hard on the brake and alighted from his mobile shop. He first took a furtive glance either side at the rear of himself, he thinks its a stick up, I reasoned that if I kept working he would speak first and I was right. By this time it appeared I was on my own the others had found cover awaiting the outcome.

'Your the fucking devil incarnate you Sampson. Every week in some form or other you jeopardise my life, aren't their enough trees on ground for you to cut up without felling more?'

'Shan't be long Mr Watson. Another half hour you'll be home. It wasn't supposed to fall this way, an your late. Your a victim of circumstances Mr Watson.'

Cutting the horizontal log was much easier than I thought and I was soon through one side in no time. Nigel and Neil had now emerged sheepishly approaching, avoiding Mr Watson's glare. I was in the rhythm, sweat was dripping from me as I heaved the axe for the last time, the three of us rolled this middle piece to the side and triumphantly turned in unison.

'Wagons Ho! Mr Watson,' we hollered 'And mind the Indians lower down.'

'You'll get Indians young Sampson. You'll get bloody Indians.' he muttered, as they trundled off and out of sight.

He was a good old stick if truth be known as was his son Ken who took over and we took less and less liberties as we grew up but there was another generation behind us, I could not speak for them.

2. First Rung of the Ladder

I left Stanley Secondary Modern to take up a job with WA Church of Southgate, Wakefield, as an apprentice plumber. I remember that first morning well. I had been told to attend at 8 am and was there 10 minutes early. I just stood about watching men milling around then getting in cars and vans and leaving. It was around 8.15 when the shop foreman asked, 'Who are you son?'

'David Sampson,' I replied, 'I was told to report here this morning.'

'Ah yes, you're Les Whitford's new mate. Les your new lad's over here.'

Suddenly this chap came towards me. 'I've been fuckin lookin for thi, come on we're late.'

I followed him through the shop and out back, to my horror we approached this enormous motorcycle. It was a 500cc Norton, my legs turned to jelly, I was petrified of motorbikes.

Les put on his helmet and mounted. 'Get on,' he grunted, 'And lean as I do!'

'It's shit or bust' I thought and climbed on.

Now Les was short and quite tubby and as the revs got louder, I wrapped my arms around him as far as I could. Then we roared off, he was crazy, or at least I thought so.

Les had just finished his National Service, he chastised me for holding on too tight and for leaning the opposite way to him on bends, to be honest he chastised me continuously for two years. 'Have you put mi tools away?' he would ask, if I answered yes, he would find one that I hadn't but it was him that was hiding them. He was a bloody good plumber but as a man he was still in the Army.

When I left school I was 5' 4" tall and weighed 6st 3lb. When our Malc left 4 years earlier, he was 5' 9" and 15st, we know who got all the buns in our house. From 15 to 17 I was to develop dramatically.

I had gone for trials at Wakefield Trinity Juniors but failed to get a start, too small was the reason.

Our Malc had already signed pro and was playing with the

second team as a prop. It was then that collectively, Malc, dad and myself decided that my food intake should change, plenty of carbohydrates and proteins, I ate like a king and all provided out of dad's pocket. Malc rigged up a punch bag from a scaffold in the back garden, barbell, weights and dumbbells were always to hand every night and at weekends. I trained and I grew.

The following year I went back to Trinity. 'What's your name son?' asked Reg Jenkinson.

'Dave Sampson sir,' I replied.

'Eh Don!' he shouted, Don Froggett emerged from the dressing room. 'This is young Sampson, remember him?'

'Certainly do. Bugger me you've grown a bit lad, go and get stripped and we'll have a look at you.'

After a few training sessions and a practice match I was signed on as a centre three-quarter. Reg and Don were ex players, passing on their knowledge and I hung on to their every word. Don was a renowned defender, he taught me front on, side on defence, then shepherding and closing down the opposition.

'Be the boss whether you're defending or attacking,' he used to say, of course this was in the time of unlimited tackles.

We had a good pack who used to dominate the scrums and a centre would receive anything up to 30 passes in a game. You could play cat and mouse with your opposite number, try the unorthodox. If you had practised it in training you had the freedom to take it into a match. Early ball to your winger, drop your winger off or dummy grubber chip kicks, it was all encouraged by the coaches.

I once remember playing against Stanley Rangers, they had started a team after I had signed for Wakefield. We were bigger, faster and fitter and that day every play came off. Gerry Mann, who played on my wing scored seven tries and we won at a canter. All credit to Stanley though, who two years later reached the Yorkshire Cup final, narrowly losing to Featherstone Juniors at Castleford. That was some achievement, I remember being a little envious, sat in the stand at Castleford watching but I couldn't have the bun and the ha'penny, I had stayed at Trinity.

The following season I represented the district side and sure enough there were several Stanley lads in the team, this broke down the barriers that had appeared to be building.

From the district, I was chosen to play for Yorkshire on the wing. This was a big honour for me. We had played and lost to Cumbria, away and the next match was against Lancashire at Castleford. By half time we were losing, Reg Jenkinson pulled the Yorkshire coach to one side and persuaded him to move me to centre. It worked, I made two decisive breaks putting Ken Huxley in under the sticks.

Ken and I were both chosen to play for England against France at Belle Vue. I was back on the wing, but thanks to Reg Jenkinson's pushing, I'd made the team. Ken and I were to team up again 10 years later at Bramley.

I remember vividly the playing of the national anthems. I stood proudly at the end of the back row alongside players like Bill Kirkbride and Jim Powe, Nia Vaughn from Cumbria, John Lowe from Warrington, Jim Russell from Huddersfield to name but a few, the list was impressive. On the other side of me was the Referee, Peter Geraghty. 'Stick wi me young un, we'll show these frogs a thing or two.' he whispered.

That was the only game I've been involved in when I knew that we would win before the game started.

Geraghty went on to referee professional rugby, most of the players turned professional too.

My life in these formative years was not all rugby, game shooting was another hobby. I remember early one evening, the sun was setting as I approached the main road, I was almost home. I had been for a walk over the fields with my beloved Canadian Cooy, my first single barrel shotgun, in fact my only ever shotgun. £15.50 from the catalogue, £1.00 deposit and £1.50 a month for two years. I was only earning about £3.00 a week as an apprentice plumber, so along with the cartridges it was quite an expensive hobby but I loved it.

I would walk miles around the adjoining countryside, pit slag heaps, corn fields, woods, anywhere to hunt game, sometimes on my own sometimes with my two brothers, Malc and Brian. They both had double barrels but they told me to get a single for my first gun.

However they didn't tell me that this was because I was quick, I'd have two birds down before they had raised their guns, so I'd been cleverly restricted without cottoning on. I was told about it some years later over a pint in the pub.

It was on this particular evening that I'd been quick to load the gun because I saw a rabbit about 20 yards in front of me. Normally so close to the main road you didn't see any game. I had been taught to always unload my gun before the road and keep it broken until I got home, which was about 100 yards over the road. Anyhow, I took aim thinking gotcha when suddenly the rabbit vanished into the hedgerow. I quietly stalked to where I thought it was but not a sign of it, so I carried on through the fence and home.

When I got inside the house, I walked into the lounge, and stood my beloved Cooy in the corner, by the cupboard. My brother Malc was sat in the chair, dad was dozing on the sofa. I walked back into the kitchen, opened the cupboard and took out my cleaning tackle, again I'd been taught always clean the gun before anything else, no excuses.

I vividly remember the click on the cupboard door as it closed and then the click of the hammer on my Canadian Cooy with the ensuing words. 'PULLLLL.' Any gun aficionado will appreciate what was going through my mind, our Malc was playing clay pigeon shooting with my Cooy. To my horror as I walked through the door, Malc had the gun raised towards the ceiling. He was sat forward on the end of the chair, his finger on the trigger, which was about two feet away from dad's head, who was still dozing on the sofa. Before Malc had finished his second 'PULLLL' then 'BOOM!' he had pulled the trigger but before that he'd cocked the hammer and before all that I'd left the bloody cartridge in my beloved Canadian Cooy.

Needless to say it came as quite a shock to my dad, still dozing he leapt off the sofa and was halfway up the stairs before he woke up. He came back into the lounge, looked at me, looked at our Malc and then the hole in the ceiling, then came the tirade of what a gormless bugger I was and my shooting days were over. Our Malc was sat in the chair still in shock. He then broke the gun and pulled out the smoking shell.

I then went on to say to our Malc and my dad, 'It's HIS fault, he shouldn't have fired it, he thought it was empty and he knows it might break the firing pin, he's told me umpteen times never ever cock and fire an empty gun.'

Dad retorted, 'It wasn't bloody empty was it, you were lucky somebody wasn't killed. Its gone through into bedroom, a might a been shot in me bed'

'But you were dozing on sofa.'

But still in shock and until the day he died, dad swore he was in bed at the time.

Further investigation of the bedroom showed the carpet piled up right under the side of the bed he normally slept in. Under the neat little mound of carpet was the splintered and shattered floorboards and under that a nice two inch clean cut hole through the lath and plaster ceiling and looking downwards into the lounge, the chair our kid was playing clay pigeon shooing on.

The consequences for me were a six-month ban from holding the gun again by dad but he insisted the hole stayed as a constant reminder and so it did for many years to come.

Dad had lifted my ban on shooting, mum had spoke up for me, 'He's paying every month for gun and can't use it! It's breaking our David's heart. He's learnt his lesson, show a bit of faith in him.' Mum had said.

Dad relented but not without a stern message about not floating off into a dreamland and disastrous consequences of being irresponsible.

Off I went, two or three times a week I would wander for miles, trespassing, poaching ducks, rabbits, hares, pigeons, I brought them all home for the pan.

Dad once joked to our Malc, 'How come if ah David's such a good shot do we get so much lead in arse end instead of its head?'

'Might a been getting dark dad when he shot these.' Malc replied.

They were taking the mickey and it brought a laugh all round.

Dad was a stickler at meal times, he would wait until Malc and I returned from training, so as a family we could all sit down and eat together. Dumplings would be the first course, followed by stewed steak, mash potatoes, two vegetables, such as swede and cabbage and onion gravy.

Sometimes mum would find another dumpling in the gravy. 'Give it our David, Leah, he needs it most.' dad would say.

This would be followed by sponge pudding and custard, or spotted dick, blackberry and apple pie or rhubarb crumble. All home made and delicious.

The daily menu was varied and dad would often say, 'This cabbage or this collie or this rhubarb is beautiful Leah,' and then with a mischievous smile say, 'Did you get it off Watson's?' (Watson's was the local greengrocer).

Mum would fire back, 'Course a did, where do you think it come from?'

In truth Joe Cook's rhubarb field skirted the east side of the estate, Watson's apple and pear orchard bottom south east, Normanton's farm was north side growing collies and cabbages, McCauley's farm west side where peas, swedes and more rhubarb was grown.

Mum rarely bought veg or fruit and dad knew it, but nothing was ever said, feeling guilty might have spoilt the taste, I supposed.

One thing mum took great satisfaction from was feeding the family, especially through our teens and apart from the traumas I constantly brought through the door those years were very special at 1 Moorhouse Avenue, especially so at Christmas.

It was Christmas 1961 and my eldest sister Connie, her husband Ken and their daughter Denise had moved next door but one, we'd cut a hole in the fence so we could pass from our garden to theirs.

Every Christmas the whole family would congregate at 1 Moorhouse Avenue. Connie, Ken and Denise, my brothers Brian with his wife Eileen and their five children, Malc with his fiancée Avis, my two sisters, Irene with her boyfriend Philip and youngest sister Maire. Together there were 18 of us congregating in an eight by six foot kitchen and a lounge which measured thirteen by ten, so you can imagine it was a bit cramped.

We dined in the lounge, the only occasion of the year. There were three sittings, the kids first, then the women, and the men last. Timing was paramount, at 11.30 am the men would gather by the back door. Once assembled dad would say, 'Malc or Brian, tell your mother we'll be back at half past two.'

'Mam we'll be back at half past two,' one of them would shout.

'Don't dare be late.' came the reply.

Now I stood right in front of my dad, he was on the top step I was on the path about six feet away. Everyone else was making their way towards the gate, I was 17 years old, I'd been working two and a half years. Every Saturday we would catch the bus to Woodlesford or Castleford for a pint, so dad would not find out, although I'm sure he knew, he must have but dad was not one for bending the rules.

'Na then ah David,' said dad, 'Just think next year tha'll be able to cum wi us.'

My heart sank a mile, 'But dad.' I protested.

'Now son niver ask anybody to break the law for thee.'

I walked back into the house, face as long as a week, all the girls were laughing, all except mum. She definitely knew I took a drink. She had cleaned up after me time and again when after beer I'd cooked bacon, egg, chips and beans, sat in front of the kitchen fire and then dropped asleep whilst reading the green final with the plate still on my knee.

She would wake me and say, 'Cummon ah David get yourself t' bed afore your dad comes down.' No mum didn't laugh, she handed me a glass and pint bottle of beer and said, 'Sup that ah David but don't tell your dad.'

'The pubs must have emptied by now,' I heard mum say, 'David go to front and see if you can see em.'

Sure enough I opened the front door and there they were, walking down the street, laughing and joking and primed up ready to fill themselves to bursting. I was allowed to sit with them, had been since I started work.

Dad would sit first and everyone quickly got to their seats. Oxtail soup to start, followed by the traditional Christmas dinner and the excitement of who'd get the other turkey leg. I'd never had one so I was full of apprehension, our Malc had got it the previous Christmas, our Brian year before, it had to my turn, I reasoned to myself.

Mum shouted from the kitchen, 'Connie ask your dad who's getting other leg will you.'

'Dad, mum wants to know who's to get the other leg this year?'

Everyone looks at dad and he proceeds to deliberate. 'Well, well, well, it's not an easy choice,' he says.

I thought, 'Course it bloody well is, I've never had one ever, in mi life.' as I stared down at the table.

'Well,' he says again followed by a long pause, 'I've given this a lot of consideration and I think it would be rude of me if I didn't ask,' he paused some more, it seemed like an age, 'Philip, yes Philip. Connie tell your mother Philip.'

Everyone cheered, as was the courteous thing, then Malc says, 'Well I knew it wouldn't be me, I got it last year.'

Then our Brian chipped in, 'And I got it year before.'

Then Ken says 'And me year before that.'

And I thought, 'Yes, if turkey had three fucking legs this year I wouldn't have got one.'

Everyone tucked in, Christmas was a very special and wonderful time in our house, mum and dad worked very hard and fully deserved such special days.

The following Christmas dad was true to his word, I got a turkey leg and partnered him at dominoes. I had been drinking with him occasionally since my 18th birthday in August but the drink on Christmas day was very special to me.

Twelve months soon comes around again, in the next year I had signed professional rugby, bought a car, was in the first team and enjoyed the company of many girlfriends. Mam would sometimes say, 'One of these days you'll bring something home you don't want to!' I think she meant a sexual disease, but she never elaborated, and I didn't dare ask.

Christmas 1963 was another eventful one for me, but what the heck so has almost every day of my life, but I did not quite expect what happened or shall I say didn't happen.

I never thought the words of a song dad used to sing to me as a child from the age of three to about nine would come back to haunt me, but they sure did. The song, a classic of the 1940's and 50's was called 'The Little Boy That Santa Claus Forgot.' One of the verses went something like this:

He wrote a note to Santa
For some soldiers and a gun
It nearly broke his little heart
When Santa didn't come
I feel sorry for that laddie....
For his hasn't got a daddy....
He's the little boy that Santa Claus forgot

The tears would run down my face and everyone had a good laugh at my expense every year. It's a wonder I didn't turn out to be paranoid at Christmas, however 1963 it was a real shock to my system. Yes, I did not receive one present all day, but then I was the guy with every-thing, I tried to keep a brave face, but gradually it hit home.

I was in the lounge and I heard Maire, my youngest sister whisper, 'Hey, has anybody bought our David anything?'

Then Connie whispered, 'Oh God! no we must do something.'

They did and I was given a big present. When I opened it, it was a big box of chocolates, something told me someone had donated one of their presents but I went along with it. I suppose I'd have been thick skinned to expect anyone to believe it didn't hurt some, it did but I'm sure there must have been a reason. It would do me more good than harm, that much dad had taught me.

It was about this time that my life in the fast lane moved up a gear, several in fact, from being on foot to becoming mobile and all the new experiences this was to bring.

'That's £533 sir, exactly.' said the rep at Comberhill Motors and I drove away 'L' plates and all, our Malc alongside.

I had signed pro forms for Wakefield Trinity £500 tax-free, dad had loaned me £33 to complete the deal, and I was the now proud owner of a brand new pale green mini, which I proudly parked outside the house. My only problem was I hadn't yet passed my driving test so could only drive if accompanied.

It was fairly late the next evening, the sun was going down, I thought, 'I'll just take it round the block.'

As I pulled up, our local bobby stepped out of the shadows. 'Been for a drive have we?'

'Yes, Officer, is there a problem?' I thought keep cool.

'What's your name son?'

'Malc,' I replied, 'Malc Sampson.'

'And do you have a driving licence Malcolm?'

'Yes officer it's in the house.'

'Then will you go in and get it?' he said.

I went in, our Malc was in the chair, 'Malc I whispered, lend us your driving licence.'

'What for?'

'Don't ask,' snapped I, 'Just lend it me.'

'Not till tha tells mi what for.' our Malc fired back.

'Because there is a copper outside who wants to see it. Cum-on.' I, pleaded.

'What copper where?' Dad chimes in.

'Oh hell,' I thought. 'Copper outside wants to see me driving licence, he's just pulled me for driving round block, an I've told him I'm our Malc, an he wants to see Licence dun he.'

'Well,' dad roared, 'Tha better go back an tell him tha's made a mistake and tha's not ah Malcolm an show him thi own licence NOW!'

Even at my age when dad raised his voice I moved, such was his presence, I duly informed the policeman that I was not our Malcolm and I was sorry.

He took the necessary particulars and did me for driving unaccompanied and not displaying L-plates (they were on the back seat).

By the time I got to court some weeks later I'd passed my test, second attempt, there was no letting go now, I was in the fast lane, wine, women and song, rugby and work. Dad would frown on my lifestyle, but I was a good trainer and I worked regular. By this time I was running my own site for WA Church's, pretty soon I was about to start courting Mavis. Life was a ball, Elvis, the Beatles, the Mecca, the clothes.

Not that much changed when I started courting, I just dropped the other women. In two years I had loved and invariably let go of dozen's, I used to be so shy and reserved.

One particular girl who caught my eye was a friend of my younger sister Maire. She was a smart good looker, lovely personality and I cared for her deeply. She was much younger than I was and I occasionally walked her home.

One Monday night I went in my bedroom to get changed when a slip of paper came under my door, it was from Maire, my younger sister had written a note saying, 'Lynn's mam and dad are coming to see mum and dad tomorrow tea.'

'Oh hell,' I thought 'I'm in for it now.'

Lynne was pregnant we hadn't been sure but this meant it must be so. Mum and dad were shocked, well dad was, I think Maire must have warned mum, but when Lynn's parents arrived you could the cut the atmosphere with a knife.

Lynn's mum was a tall imposing woman, her dad was only tiny, but neither were very happy. Mum was courteous as a person could be in the circumstances. I sat in the chair head bowed, listening intently. Dad sat opposite in what was known as the 'shotgun chair' bloody appropriate I remember thinking.

Dad had not spoken, and we all listened intently to Mr and Mrs Holdroyd. 'Did you know she was only sixteen last week? Do you know we could have you locked up?'

I could see the temperature rising. 'We'll get married,' I replied thinking naively that's what everyone else on estate does.

Oops! The temperature went higher, Lynn's mum's voice raised even higher, retorted, 'Marry, marry at 16, she'll be marrying no one. Doctor Merrick's already said by the time she's 20 she'll probably have four kids.'

I remember thinking to myself, they're blaming me for other three. Then dad had to put his two penneth in.

'Couldn't tha av used summat ah David n tha owt t' av more sense.'

I fired back, 'Don't you start dad, you've never told me owt about sex.'

Dad looked straight back at me in shock, yes I'd hit home, he was speechless but I instantly regretted belittling him in front of mum and the Holdroyds. However it did bring a bit of calm into the confrontation.

I repeated, 'I will marry her and she knows I will we think the world of each other.'

Mr Holroyd who had hardly spoken a word suddenly stood up, 'She's not marrying and certainly not to a Don-Jo-Ann like thee.'

'Well then I'll pay what it takes for its upbringing.'

Mrs Holdroyd then asserted, 'You'll pay nowt, it's going to be adopted and that's last word on the matter. Good day to you Leah, George.' and they vanished.

I saw them occasionally in the village, but they never spoke to me again, ever.

Lynn had the baby, a boy. I was told by my sister Maire and Mavis, who later became my wife. They saw him at birth, and a few days later he was taken away. I was never to see him or know of his whereabouts and still after all these years I have never stopped hoping he might just turn up, even it was only to say hello and listen to my side of events.

As for Lynn I've only been in her company once since then at our Maire's fortieth birthday, 23 years later. She was with her husband and we never spoke. I felt awkward and aggrieved that Maire hadn't warned me Lynn would be there.

I still ask myself 'Has Lynn ever met our son? Does he know of us, is he okay?' Haunting daily questions.

Lynn's younger brother, John started coming in my pub, the Ship, some years later, and often we would train with the pub soccer team. John was a very talented player, but this particular tackle on me, his first ever, seemed to have a bit of vengeance in it. I later had a quiet word.

We went on to play rugby league together and have been life long friends ever since. His friendship has a special value to me. He's too old to be my son, I know that but perhaps that's what I've been dealt and possibly I never will see my son with Lynn, maybe that's the penance we have to pay, but we were only kids.

I take strength when I look at my three children, Dean, Jonty and Becky and my grandchildren Olivia and Joe. Fate sent me on this particular road and on these occasions I've felt Shangri-la is just around the corner.

3. Trinity Days

I signed professional forms in April 1963. Trinity were at Wembley versus Wigan a month later, a great game, Trinity won 25-10 and our Malc scored the first try. It had been a fairy tale come true for him, he'd missed two Wembley finals in 1960 and 61 because of a hand injury, sustained in a car accident two nights after the 1960 semi-final. He had missed two and a half seasons, made a come back and his nineteenth consecutive game was at Wembley, as I say, a fairy tale.

Come pre-season 1963-64 he had counselled me to create an early impression on the then coach, Ken Trail. 'Don't let the older players hold you back, go for gold in everything you do,' he advised, which I did, including some titanic sprints against Don Metcalfe for the last 300 yards of a five mile run over Heath Common.

As soon as we hit the front door of the Graziers pub, Don would start the sprint to Trinity's ground at Belle Vue, full throttle. I always won but never by more than the thickness of a training vest. Don was 31, I was 19 but I could tell by Ken's comments and eye contact, he was impressed.

The start of the season couldn't come quick enough for me, I was chosen as centre for the seconds at home versus Hull A-team and my first meeting with a Hull legend opposite. Terry Hollindrake the opposing centre was a 6' 2" big stepping former England winger and renowned for his ability to crash tackle man and ball. Little did I know that a few years hence we would be teammates and little did he know that I had decided to take some advice as to my pre-match warm up.

At that time it constituted simply stretching and short sprints, 10 yards this way, 10 yards jog, 10 yards sprint but that day each time I stepped and changed direction, I swapped the ball in my arms and instinctively raised the bent elbow of the other arm. I was performing for Terry and he was watching, we won and I scored two tries, I realised that I had out-psyched him because he never came near me until the final whistle, when he offered his hand and congratulated me, 'Well played young Sampson, keep it up.'

On reaching the touchline my elder brother Brian approached me, 'I told you it would work.' he had been my councillor, however I was soon to forget this wisdom at great cost.

I played one more A-team game the following week and then the bombshell dropped. Ken Trail called me over during training, 'Big Neil's not fit for Saturday, you'll be starting at 4. Best of luck! Run with us for the rest of training.'

I didn't need telling, it was Hunslet at Parkside, first round of the Yorkshire Cup. Their two centres were Geoff Shelton and Alan Preece, an awesome combination.

From Thursday right up to kick off, I can only say that apart from the pride and excitement that goes with the occasion, I was full of trepidation. Now that is a polite way of saying I was shitting myself, I knew there would be no way of out-psyching Shelton and Preece or anyone else for that matter. This was going to be an incredible 80 minutes.

That Saturday morning my dad instructed my mum 'Leah, knock our David summat to settle his stomach, he's bloody white.'

Mum appeared with a glass tumbler from the kitchen. 'Drink it straight down.'

It was a raw egg beaten up with half a glass of sherry, I duly did as I was told then lay on the settee to nap. I never did drop off as I could hear dad's voice in the kitchen telling people who came to the house, family, friends, the insurance man, whoever, 'Keep the noise down, our David's asleep in t'other room.' He meant well, he was very proud of all of us but he never pushed it down anyone's throat.

Five minutes to kick off and I felt okay. Rubbing shoulders in the changing rooms with the likes of Turner, Vines and Wilkinson would make anyone feel good and the man on my wing was Oupa Coetzer, a great and highly respected South African winger. He was the first to wish me luck and was followed by every other player in the room. 'Good luck young Sammy.' was ringing in my ears as I trotted out, I heard Derek Turner say to the forwards, 'Just remember lads, 90 fuckin quid, that's ours today. Do you hear?'

I'd been so overwhelmed it never occurred to me about the money, 90 quid was a fortune to a 19 year old in 1963.

The first couple of minutes there were some torrid forward exchanges but Wakefield were well known for getting the ball wide quickly, sure enough the ball was not long in coming my way. Before the game I had decided to give Coetzer some early quick passes, he was strong and that's how he liked it, it would take the attention away from me and maybe result in a bit of space.

Now, as I remember it, it went like this. Harold Poynton to Ken Hirst, Ken on to me, it would not be in my hands long enough to pick up sweat before it was in Oupa's then BANG! I'd been hit by a train. It was late as were most trains in those days, I was down, must get up, must get up were my only thoughts through the mist, or was it steam? I rose to my feet. Our Brian's words, 'Don't ever let them know they've hurt you,' echoed in my mind as I looked forward to see Oupa Coetzer bundled into touch on the corner flag 50 yards up field but I was hurt, my shoulder was broken, clean as a whistle and I knew it. So did Paddy Armour, our Physio. 'Sorry young Sampson, you're off, cummon.'

The game had not stopped and from the resultant scrum, Hunslet's Dave Smith, their winger was coming up the touchline. Instinctively I pulled away from Paddy and set to cut him off when a voice bellowed, 'Leave the bastard, he's mine!' as Derek (Rocky) Turner passed me and together with Gerry Round, clattered him into touch.

As Paddy led me over the touch and along the long walk around the pitch I thought to myself, 'Welcome to the big misters game.' Tears streamed down my face, the occasion, the emotion, the atmosphere. A full house, screaming and baying, it all came out and there were no subs then, 12 against 13 I reflected as the ambulance took me to St James' Hospital. Another figure of eight, I knew only too well as I'd broken both shoulders previously as a junior.

Coming back in the ambulance the radio was on, my ears pricked up, 'Hunslet 9 Trinity 9,' Yes! We get another bite of the cherry. I could cope with the pain of the injury but Derek Turner's words when I got back hurt more, 'Get that elbow up in future young Sammy!' Of course he was right, the golden rule had slipped my mind, if only it had been Terry Hollindrake on the opposing wing not a stocky insignificant winger called Dave Smith. I had dropped my guard and paid the price, no complaints, it's all part of being a gladiator.

We lost the replay the following Wednesday but I kept the Green Final cutting from the Saturday night paper. Its headline, full print on the back page, 'Sampson's £30-a-minute.' I had not realised an away draw was winning money, nor had I realised that I'd been on the field three minutes.

It had taken eight weeks for my shoulder to heal. I had played one A-team game on that eighth weekend to the day and Ken Trail came to me in training, 'Young Sammy,' he uttered, 'Train wi' first team this week I'll probably play you right centre at Keighley on Saturday, all right?'

'Yes fine.' I replied.

'Oh an train wi' first team from now on unless I say different.'

I was elated, I felt 10 feet tall. I remember it well because not only did I complete the whole game but also I put my winger Fred Smith in for a couple of tries. On one occasion I had comfortably rounded my opposite number, a certain Brain Todd a highly talented centre and much older than myself.

Each week passed and Ken Trail would say, 'You're on wing this week, Bramley at home.' Then the following week, 'You're full back, Hull at Hull,' and so on. Stand off against Halifax, right centre against St. Helens, left centre against Warrington. I didn't care, I was learning and growing in confidence. Two tries at home against Leeds thanks to Harold Poynton, 'Just run for the gap!' he had barked. Suddenly, with not a hand laid on me, I was scoring, such was his skill.

One of the highlights of my first season was Leeds away on Boxing Day. I was marking the legendary Louis Jones, one of dad's idols, I received a few press lines commenting on how sound and capable I had looked in such exalted company.

When everyone was fit, I was on the sub's bench. I could not expect more, the team's backs were a who's who of rugby. 'No rush.' dad would reassure me.

The following season was similar, I was disappointed to miss out on selection for the Yorkshire Cup final at Fartown because I had played there a few weeks previously alongside 'Mr Smith' who was a new trialist. I can remember Ken Trail introducing me to him on the bus as 'Smith, he hasn't played much rugby, just a bit of rugby union, look after him an' teach him all you can up to kick off.'

'Oh well,' I thought, 'he's just another trialist, they come and go, strange for him to be in the first team though.'

We ran out onto the pitch and I knew that there was something different about this guy, he didn't run like the rest of us he bounced, he pranced, I couldn't help but feel inquisitive. 'We would soon see,' I thought.

The game was about 10 minutes old, I hadn't given Smith the ball because we were on the back foot all the time, when suddenly, I received a pass, Mr Smith was not on his wing, he had somehow strayed inside, he was in space but flat-footed. I thought, 'Here, you take it you've done nothing so far.'

He caught the ball and froze.

'Run!' I bellowed and 'WHOOSH', he launched himself. He ran from our 25, around Brian Curry the Huddersfield full back and placed the ball under the sticks in what seemed like 5 seconds flat.

Players and fans alike recognised that this was no ordinary 'A N Other' announced on the tannoy before kick-off. Half time came and it was broadcast, in our changing room only, 'Smith' was none other than Berwyn Jones, Olympic 4x100 relay World Record holder, I feel I can say without fear of contradiction that Berwyn was the fastest man ever to play our beloved game and I gave him his first ever pass. I played alongside him many times, he was quick to learn and had plenty of heart, he scored some memorable tries, none better than a short range squeeze, in on the corner at Belle Vue against St. Helens for us to win 5-4.

To train with Berwyn was equally as inspirational as it was soul destroying. When we sprinted, he did his strides, or bounding, it was like being overtaken by a kangaroo. Unfortunately Berwyn came to rugby league in his mid 20's, had he been introduced earlier or gained experience as I did as a teenager, he would surely have made the hall of fame, but then on reflection if I'd had his pace, so might I.

My most disappointing moment at Trinity was being selected as substitute at Headingley in the Challenge Cup semi-final against Hunslet. We lost narrowly. Tony Thomas got the nod, 'More experience' Ken Trail explained, Berwyn played right wing and I felt that a couple of well executed kicks from him might just have broken them down and produced something.

The tactical kick was not as prevalent in the 60's as today, although that was certainly because of unlimited tackles but it did not discourage the likes of Fred Smith, who's ability to chip and chase was legendary in those days and many times I saw the great Neil Fox use this ploy.

In those two seasons I competed in about 50 games for Trinity but fate was just around the corner, a pre-season game in August 1965 resulted in torn ankle ligaments, it was so bad it virtually wrote my season off.

The following summer during pre-season training, Mr Stuart Hatfield, the Chairman, came on to the training pitch and called myself and Terry Hopwood across. 'I've arranged for you to transfer to Bramley, it's not negotiable, the deal is done.'

Mr Hatfield was a coal merchant and was blunt and abrasive, I had never liked him since he chastised me for scoring the winning try against Dewsbury. I had dummied to Oupa Coetzer and scored, Mr Hatfield's reasoning was that he had paid a lot of money for Oupa and he was out there to score the tries. This dressing down took place in front of the whole team, he went on to reproach others but not the big name players.

It came to mind what dad had once told me, 'Never let a bully get top side,' so I had to have my moment. I pulled Mr Hatfield in the corridor and quietly made the point that in my opinion he was being very unfair. Oupa might not have scored, I'd made a split second decision, if I hadn't scored from it he would have every right to reprimand me but as it was I expected praise and encouragement when due, otherwise my decision making would be clouded by his interference.

By this time Mr Hatfield was crimson, I thought he was going to explode. Ken Trail intervened, 'Come on young Sammy, out training, you're late.'

As I made my way out Ken whispered, 'Standing up for right is commendable but don't be surprised if there's a backlash, he's an Elephant.'

'Fuck him,' I thought, 'He screwed our Malc out of some money, he'd screwed me out of money and now he wanted to tell me how to play, I'd broken my shoulder giving an early ball to Oupa at Hunslet so if the opposition were going to take the dummies, I was going to give them.' Anyway, in conclusion, I never got another chance. I was due 500 quid for 20 games in a season, I was on 18 and it never went to 19.

Malc had explained to dad what had happened after training. 'Ah David,' he'd sighed, 'In principle that was right but at times discretion is the better part of valour son, but what's done is done.'

I couldn't help but feel that Mr Hatfield enjoyed his ultimatum to Terry and myself, all it did for me was to steel my resolve to prove him a buffoon. My stubborn resolve was obviously inherent, something that must have been a definitive characteristic which Dad turned into a positive on the building sites of years gone by.

In 1964-65 our Malc had bought a piece of land in Lee Moor from Alf Hanks and started building Avis and himself a dream home, all the family would muck in and dad was at the forefront.

This particular Saturday the house had reached the stage of topping out, this meant that the gable's scaffolding was at its highest. Malcolm and Ken were walling bricks, dad was labouring taking up mixing after mixing, he was in his mid 50's and hadn't been on a building site since 1935 or 36 some 30 years. Now his weekends were helping to secure Malc and Avis a future. I was helping too but was soon to feel inadequate, as we all did, when dad who had spent 10 minutes pottering about, or so I thought, suddenly placed a square piece of three quarter inch plywood on his head, it was about 15 inches square and he was trying to balance it and walk keeping it flat. On further inspection, there was a piece of sponge with a hole in the middle on the underside, this he said cushioned to the shape of his crown when the weight went on. I tried it on, it hurt without any weight but I was inquisitive, I put a couple of bricks on the board and tried to balance them but I had to use one hand to steady it. I then attempted to scale the pole ladder but like with a hod you needed both hands free, the board fell off my head. 'Forget it ah David.' dad instructed, he then stacked eight bricks on and scaled the ladder with it on his head, the next time with 10 bricks and so on.

All day he stacked out that top lift and the others. He had enthralled us at lunch time with stories about 'tupping' for that's what he called it. In the late 1920's and early 30's, his boss, old Alf Hanks would wager bets that dad was the 'Top Tupper' in this region and often won money gambling in building site rivalry.

Dad said, 'I had an advantage, I was always carrying two more bricks than my nearest rival, if he put eight on his board I would put 10, if he put 10 I would put 12, if anybody put 12 it would then be down to speed and stamina and I'd plenty of that as well.' he had declared.

Now bricks in those days were Armitage best weighing about 8 1/2 lbs each. Dad had added his best was 14 but that was to get top side of one opponent called Farrar from Thorpe, who was very strong. I later realised looking at dad on an old photo his neck was same width as his head, I now knew why.

Alf Hanks had got dad drunk that night on free beer in the Miners but he always professed caution, however I thought I knew better, even in beer.

It was a Sunday night, I had been drinking with the lads at the Miners before going to see Mavis, we had been courting for some time. I was late and got a roasting so I stormed out and went to Heppy's Fish Restaurant on Denby Dale Road. I was driving my new car a Vauxhall VX 490, British Racing Green with a white flash, bench seats and column change and I was speeding. I was approaching a 40 mph zone so I eased off the pedal, good job I did, I could see this big old Cambridge on my right up ahead at the junction.

He won't? He can't? He did! Pulled out straight into my path. I braked, swerved and hit him broadside, bounced over the verge, through the hedge, down an embankment finally coming to rest in a back garden.

The bench seat had come in handy, I had dropped onto it but my face had hit the dashboard. I climbed out, 'Only a few cuts and bruises,' assured the lady who took me into her house 'You'll be OK.'

'Thanks,' I replied. 'Can you get me a taxi please?'

Other people had looked after the other chap, it turned out he had a broken hip and the police prosecuted him for driving without due care. If I hadn't slowed down neither of us would have made it. I felt invincible, I was caught up in the fast lane thinking only of myself, it was selfish but I saw it differently back then.

Ironically, I found out later Heppy's was closed on Sundays.

4. Special Day Special Woman

The saying goes behind every successful man is a woman, a special woman in my case. I really don't think my wife Mavis knew what she was letting herself in for when the words 'For better or for worse' were uttered during our wedding vows because even on that day we went straight into the fast lane and she's been my co-driver ever since, 35 years come December 2001.

Even on our wedding day, Bramley had asked, begged me to play against Leeds at Headingley and Mavis went along with it. We were to drive on to Harrogate after the match and stay overnight at the Granby then up to Kendal the next day.

It was a disaster from start to finish. I'd been out the night before, as you did. My car was in dock so I'd borrowed our Malc's Austin Cambridge then broke the exhaust pipe. Dad was livid with me for being late in so he wasn't going to the wedding. I managed to get Alva Palfreyman to weld the exhaust up but our Malc had taken the dogs for a walk. He thought we were getting married at 12 but it was actually 11 so he missed it.

We dashed to Leeds after the speeches, the press had a field day and I had a stinker, I really was in no condition to face Syd Hynes and Alan Smith that day and well they knew it.

From Headingley we drove on to the Granby, I was shattered on arriving and the last thing I wanted was hassle but sure enough I got some. We booked in and put our bags in the room only to find to our dismay that there were two single beds six feet apart, Mavis was horrified. Like a gallant knight I pushed the two beds together but it was all too much for Mavis. She had made concessions all day and this was just too much, she sat on the edge of the bed and started to cry.

'OK, OK,' I soothed, 'I'm off down to sort it out.'

I explained at reception but they didn't have anything else, they apologised but two thirds of the hotel was closed at that time of year and they couldn't help us.

A chap who had been reading his newspaper nearby, the Times I'd noted, stood up and approached the desk.

'Excuse me,' he asserted 'I couldn't help overhearing your predicament and I'd like to help. Mine is a lovely double room overlooking the Stray, it's at your disposal.'

He addressed the receptionist, 'See to it young man and shame on you and your hotel.'

He turned back to me, 'Perhaps you would bring your good lady down, we'll have a tipple before dinner and it will give them chance to prepare your room.'

I returned to Mavis and related the story and invitation, it put the smile back on her face. We had a couple of drinks and thanked the chap for such kindly consideration then went to dinner. The meal and wine were superb but I was absolutely exhausted after it and suggested that we retired to our room. I climbed into bed whilst Mavis went into the bathroom, that was a mistake.

'What time is it?' I rolled over and asked.

'2 o'clock' Mavis said, 'You were fast asleep when I came out of the bathroom.'

The sound of a dog had woken me, barking loudly and incessantly. 'It's kept me awake,' Mavis moaned.

I answered, 'Good dog, it's woke me up. All's well that ends well.'

We then proceeded on for a short stay in Shangri-la.

5. Our Denise

Denise as a youngster had shown exceptional talent as a runner, winning school championships by frightening margins. She was also a talented ballet dancer, the discipline for which would stand her in good stead in later years for long heartbreaking hours of travelling and training.

At the tender age of 11, her local teacher Mrs Roberts recognised that my sister Connie and her husband Ken had produced a child of singular talent. Denise had obviously inherited her grandmother's genes through the loving partnership of her mum and dad. We have no need to look too far back on Ken's side of the family either, his father was well renowned as a runner of note.

When discussing this subject my dad once told of when they used to go to gambling schools over the Fenton Fields every Sunday. If the police raided, nobody was as quick as little Willy Ramsden. 'He niver got copt.'

We had first hand knowledge of the genetic lineage, for Ken's father was also a miner.

Mrs Roberts had suggested to Ken that he take Denise to an athletics club. Her first year with Wakefield Harriers at 11 years old she competed in the 11 to 15 juniors group, she came second in the Yorkshires and second in the Yorkshire schools.

It was at this time that she met the Olympic silver medallist, Dorothy Hyman. Dorothy persuaded Connie and Ken to let Denise join Hickleton Main track club. It meant more travelling for Ken but he unselfishly threw himself into the fray and 12 months later Denise was a champion. Yorkshire Champion, Yorkshire Schools Champion, England Schools Champion and National Coal Board Champion. She also came a close third in both the Inter-Counties National Championships and the Northern Counties over 100 and 150 yards, a feat she was to emulate the following year, raising her standards yet again.

In 1966, Denise made a clean sweep, first place in all events, voted top national female junior sprinter. Her grandad (Sampson that is) gave her ten bob after winning one particular championship, the All England Counties. He had scribbled a little message and rolled it up inside the ten bob note, it read, 'I hope this doesn't make you a professional but I'm the proudest grandad in the world.'

For the first time Denise had beaten two girls who had beaten her in both the previous two years.

England had won the World Cup. I had signed for Bramley. Mavis and I married that December. I remember life was pretty good at that time.

Denise continued to make us all very proud of her, 1967 representing England in Canada at the age of 15. Winning the 100 yards in 10.4 seconds, wind assisted, in the 15 to 19 age group. A UK all time list record for women.

Come 1968 she ran in the 15 to 17 age group, winning all before her, obtaining the title 'Top National Intermediate Sprinter' and making the qualifying time for the Mexico Olympics 100 metres in a time of 11.6.

I certainly wasn't challenging her in those days although I had enjoyed the contest of sprinting against her previously. This had been a one-off occasion, a jovial boast on my part to Ken, Denise's dad, that he shouldn't underestimate me.

'What?' he'd quipped, 'You're not serious? You're not quick enough to beat her.'

'Right,' I retorted, 'I'll take her on, I'll come training.'

The epic meeting took place at the Castleford track where she occasionally trained.

'It's uphill,' I remember commenting to Ken. 'Can't we sprint down hill?'

'No, in training we run uphill. Do some stretching and exercising with Denise and then it's sprint time.'

The only other person in the stadium was my sister Connie, she had the stopwatch and stood near the finish line. I had opted for the inside lane. I remember informing Ken 'I can already taste that pint' for that was the wager.

'Take your marks,' Ken was being very official about it all. 'Set, Go.'

He had even brought a starting pistol.

Inside 10 metres Denise was already a metre up on me, 'Relax and accelerate,' I thought. At 50 metres I had made up the difference. It was nip and tuck at 75 metres as I heard Connie shout, 'Come on Denise!' I pipped her at the finish.

I had surprised even myself and although I wasn't short of confidence, I had been unsure of the outcome.

Denise was already on her way back to the start for the next sprint, Ken had a slight look of shock on his face. I walked down to the start, Denise wasn't even breathing heavy.

I needed more time. 'Just let me adjust my laces Ken,' I pretended to refasten my lace, then for the second time. 'To your marks. Set. BANG.'

This time Denise was off even quicker. I powered forward to make up the leeway, which once again I did, to win by a whisker.

I was now sucking air through every orifice in my body as I made my way back to the start. 'Suck it in, deep breaths.' I was telling myself as I lined up alongside Denise.

Ken's voice came over once again, 'Set. BANG.'

I was much slower off the mark this time, Denise was gone, 30 metres, I simply ran off the track. 'I need more recovery time,' I pleaded.

I overheard Ken say to Denise, 'That's three, seven more and we'll take Uncle David home, you should be warm now, don't lose the intensity.'

She hadn't opened up yet. I stood by Connie as Denise did her 10th sprint, a card she was holding showed all to be under 12 seconds. I enjoyed my pint and the lesson it taught me. I wasn't fit enough, at that time we rarely did 100 metre sprints absolute maximum, and believe me I was at absolute maximum.

Dad was very proud of his granddaughter's achievements to date. Spending many summer days and evenings travelling in support of her, in exactly the same way as he had continued with Malc and myself. Quietly enjoying his summer weekends, Saturday or Sunday or both, travelling around the country with Connie, Ken and Denise, watching her burn up the track with ever increasing pace. Meet to meet, year after year.

It was a beautiful summer Saturday. I had accompanied dad to Cleckheaton for the Yorkshire Spring Championships. We clambered out of the car and in the blink of an eye dad had lit up a cig.

He hadn't spoke for the last five or ten minutes. His cheeks sank into his face as he took a huge draw followed by a deep sigh as he exhaled. 'By I needed that ah David,' he followed, 'There's a pub just around the corner. We'll see you later Ken. Are we going to win Denise?'

'I'll do my best grandad,' came the reply.

'Can't ask for more,' dad called as we turned the corner.

Dad knew the best pubs near almost every athletics track in the country. He was on his second cigarette as we sat down with a pint and he proceeded to tell me that he always found somewhere 'Just for a couple' he would say 'to sleck mi clek,' he then lit up another cig.

I'd noticed the way he had attacked his cigarette packet since getting out of the car but not once had he lit up during the journey. 'Going a bit heavy on cigs aren't you dad?'

'Well I can't smoke in car might affect our Denise so I'm dying for one when we reach our destination. I'll settle down in a couple of mins.'

We had another drink and a sandwich followed by a stroll in the sunshine back to the stadium. We took our seats near to the finish line. Dad removed his trilby, put on his glasses and proceeded to scan the programme giving me inside information as to the prowess of several athletes at the meeting.

It was a wonderful atmosphere the announcers voice the cheering I noticed Denise warming up. I had only seen her a couple of times on TV.

I commented 'Denise looks much more powerful these days dad.'

'Yes your right son. Training for Olympics last year did that. I think she's going to do well today.'

The Olympics had given her a new air of confidence. Although the British team did not win they had broken the Commonwealth 100 metre relay record.

Denise contested her heats and finals with a cool seemingly

calculated efficiency but the celebration came when the announcer stated that Denise had a winning time for the 200 metres final of 23 seconds a new record.

On hearing this Ken had calmly turned to Connie, 'I told you it was quick.'

'Yes love you did you told me it was quick.'

Denise was particularly pleased this was her fifth consecutive Yorkshire Championship. Also, only weeks later she attained the Northern Counties titles. Her record for the 200 metres on that beautiful summer's afternoon still stands to this day.

Unfortunately when running in the UK Nationals in Cardiff, Denise was to suffer an injury which forced premature retirement. However, she was to marry Melvyn my mate and they produced Stephen and later Gemma, Stephen being born just a couple of weeks after her beloved grandad Sampson passed away. Along with her mum, my dad was her greatest fan.

Stephen now attends Cardiff University and Gemma is carving out a modelling career, both originate of quality mining stock.

Ken unfortunately passed away in the summer of 1999.

Connie her mum is at present in Canada, Prince Edward Island, nursing our sister Maire who is sadly very ill. She is only 54.

Maire and John have two grandchildren and although so far away they are always in my thoughts. Our overseas seeds of hope.

Irene my other sister sadly split from Phil in an acrimonious divorce. Phil remarried and has another wife and family. His and Irene's two girls have both grown up and are career teachers. Carol working for many years in Spain. Gill in various parts of the world.

Ironically, Irene now lives on the Moorhouse Estate. We do not get together too many times as a family and that is sad, but when seeds are sown and the harvest reaped, not all are guaranteed a trip to Shangri-la.

6. Brotherly Love

The sun was beating down, we had learned on the radio it was the hottest day of the year. We as a family were on the beach at our favourite resort Filey. The children were still young but growing fast. Avis, Mavis and Maire were sun bathing, each had a deck chair (no expense spared). Malc, John and myself were entertaining the children in the shallows. The two dogs Dell and Rex lay in the shade of the chairs we had left unoccupied.

The beach was packed as was the promenade. The ice-cream vendors were struggling to cope with the demand. The aroma of hot dogs wafted on to the beach by a warm gentle breeze.

As we returned to base, 'Where are the dogs?' I asked. 'They were there a minute ago. John you take the beach that way, Malc and I will cover this way and the prom.'

We began to weave our way through the throng of people asking as we progressed towards the cobbled ramp. 'Have you seen two Golden Lab's? Excuse me, have you seen two Golden Lab's?' We continually repeated, in between giving a whistle and a call 'Dell Dell Rex Rex.'

Malc veered up the ramp, I continued on the beach for a few yards. It was unusual for the dogs to stray. We had walked them on the beach that morning for miles they had enjoyed splashing in the breakers, we only cut over the cliffs because Dell insisted on lapping up seawater. It had been a long walk, we were tired so it seemed fair to assume so were the dogs.

Suddenly I heard our Malc's whistle, I looked up he was halfway down the cobble ramp waving me to come over. I quickly jogged across to find he had seen Dell on top of the prom about 50 yards further on.

He was a little agitated I'd noticed but without giving it another thought I jogged up the ramp. On top there were literally hundreds of people milling about, some were sat on benches, some laid out sunning themselves on the grass, others leaning on the sea wall. But all seemed to be looking in the same direction to some sort of commotion over on my right. Some were sniggering, others laughing and some with a genuine look of concern.

I proceeded to scan for Dell, 'Here boy, here boy,' I shouted. Dell turned and headed for me.

Just as he did this chap came bursting towards me, 'Hey you, you. Is that your bloody dog?'

I was mortified by what I saw, no bloody wonder our Malc had done a runner. He was big and I mean big.

A little lady who I presumed was his wife started screaming 'Just look at what he's done. Look what he's done. Your dog. Your bloody dog,' she was shouting in one ear.

He was spluttering 'The fucking thing. The fucking thing.'

'Look I am sorry, just tell me what I can do to make amends.'

His white shirt and his trousers were covered in dog shit. Not run of the mill shit but orange/tan coloured slime. 'Drinking seawater gives them diarrhoea' our Malc had mentioned earlier in the day and poor old Dell must have been caught short. I was puzzled how this much damaged had been done, however I wasn't likely to find out from this couple the mood they were in.

I offered to lend him clothes and take his to the cleaners, I offered him money, I got fed up apologising to no avail. One or two people nearby started to put their two penny worth in so I turned on them, 'It's nowt to do with you so bugger off.' This seemed to work.

I made a final apology and turned away. I reached the bottom of the cobbles, spun to shout Dell who was getting too far behind. I still remember their silhouettes in the setting sun.

When I reached Malc, John and the rest everyone was laughing. I thanked our kid for setting me up, 'I nearly got lynched up there.'

'I hid at the bottom of the cobble until I knew it was OK' he quipped. 'It is your dog and I saw him shit on that bloke. I wasn't carrying the can.'

'I knew something was wrong when you sent me up for him but never dreamt. But how did it get all over him?'

'Well,' our kid say's 'They were both asleep, laid on their backs. I saw Dell having a sniff, the guy had a newspaper on his face and Dell shit on the paper. He woke, jumped up and all the shit ran off the newspaper onto him. That's when I scarpered.'

I don't know if he's still alive but if he is and reads this I can only say sorry once again. I hope after all this time he can see a funny side to it.

7. It's a Set Up

1968 was not only a good year for me on the rugby field, it was also the year that dad and I patched up our differences.

Filey was the resort where Malc, our Maire's husband John and myself once again decided to take a break. This particular weekend we had all booked in the Beach Hotel on the front, somehow Mavis had persuaded me to take Dean for a pre-breakfast pushchair stroll up the prom.

As I remember, the sun was trying to break through an early morning haze. A vague lone figure up ahead caught my eye. He was sat on a bench reading a newspaper. He was a good 100 yards ahead but there was no mistaking it was dad. If he'd been a mile away, mist and all, he would have been instantly recognisable. As I got nearer and nearer I was thinking, 'I've been set up, this has been planned,' but I never considered turning back and I knew I couldn't walk past.

Dad hadn't met Dean before and I approached heart in mouth. Dad looked up as I was only a few feet away to his right, he removed his glasses and spoke, 'I'm beginning to think I've been set up ah David.'

'Yeah same here dad.'

'Is this ah Dean then?'

'This is him dad.'

'Lift im aht, let's ev odd.'

Dean was just one year old. I sat alongside dad as he cradled and amused Dean. The mist began to lift and the sun came bursting through.

A few minutes later Maire, John and Jane, Malc, Avis and Lee appeared with Mavis sheepishly bringing up the rear. Nothing was said, nothing discussed, dad and I never crossed words again. It was the day I grew up more than any other previous.

Now dad could be stubborn, positively unreasonable at times, he had always refused to give me the key of the door, even when I was 21. Dad would contend that if you were out after 12 o'clock you were up to no good, we'd had several run in's over this but he was unbending. 'It's my house and they're my rules.' So even when Mavis and I had married and were living with mum and dad the rules still applied but only if I was out on my own.

On the night in question I was out celebrating Dean's birth, wetting the baby's head. Mavis was still in the hospital. I was late home. I was locked out. I sat on the wall outside the house, if I waited long enough, mum would come down and let me in, she always did and sure enough this time she did the same but I had come to a decision too. 'Don't lock it mum, I'm not stopping.' I packed a suitcase and left telling mum not to worry, I was going to Mavis' mum's.

I had spent all 23 years of my life at 1 Moorhouse Avenue but I never slept there again. What should have been a joyous occasion had been soured. For 12 months dad and I hadn't spoken to each other until that misty morning on the sea front at Filey.

On reflection as the years rolled by dad's 'do as I say, not as I do' attitude mellowed, but I came to believe that in my case he recognised the latent talent I possessed, and he was also trying to protect me from myself. Furthermore I think he was frustrated at his inability to communicate with me enough for me to knuckle down and conform.

Mum used to say, 'Ah David is just like his dad,' maybe that was dad's problem. Maybe he recognised the fact and didn't want me to follow the same path. I'm sure he wanted more for all of us.

1968 was also a particular pleasing year for Mavis and myself, we had settled into our new house a three storey mid terrace in Lofthouse, Number 3 Temple View.

Dean was walking and the neighbours were wonderful it had to have some significance that I was playing the best rugby of my career. I had made the Yorkshire Shadow Squad and when you remember at that time Dick Gemmell, Syd Hynes, Neil Fox, Ian Brook and Geoff Wrigglesworth were my contemporaries.

When I read the Yorkshire Post and saw my name I felt I could further my career, if only one of the big clubs would come in for me.

I had matured both physically and mentally. This particular season we had taken the scalps off all four challenge cup semi-finalists away from home. Each match had been under floodlights, it was ironic that Wakefield, my old club were to visit Wembley only two years after I'd been told by Stuart Hatfield that I was leaving for Bramley.

In the 1965/66 season, I had torn ankle ligaments in a pre season match, been out until after Christmas and apart from half a game against Hull, I had not made the first team.

How fate works in odd ways. Maybe if they had persevered I too would have been in the famous water splash final between Wakefield and Leeds. I had subbed against Hunslet in the 1964/65 semi-final which we lost. I remembered how I felt cheated and it was only a newspaper report on the war in Vietnam which brought me back to reality. Just get on with it I thought.

Castleford later came for me but Bramley botched that deal, so Castleford signed Tony Thomas from Trinity. Castleford then went to Wembley two years on the trot in 1969 and 1970. I hadn't killed a robin I'd shot a flock. When Castleford came back for me almost 10 years on, it wasn't the 13 1/2 stone centre they signed but a 16 stone prop, well better late than never.

During my early and mid 20's I used to drink with dad in either the Ship Inn or the Miners Arms. Jack and Maureen had been the licensees of the Miners at that time. Jack was a Moorhouse lad, his younger brother Alan was the same age as me and had been a lifelong friend, although we had blacked each others eyes on occasions.

Jack and Maureen ran the pub so well I'd often say to Jack that I'd like a pub and occasionally he would allow me to pull a few pints. Jack and Maureen ran the pub for about three years but Jack also worked down the pit. It must have been tough for them both.

When I was about 27 years old, I'd tried selling with British Oxygen but I decided I wanted a pub. Mavis was petrified at the thought but decided to give it a try. We put our names down and then sought Jack's advice. 'If the brewery are convinced that Mavis wants a pub then you'll get one,' he stated. So the strategy was that Mavis would bombard the brewery boss by phone.

Both the Ship and the Miners had come on the market, 'We want the Miners,' I'd insisted, it was still my local.

The current landlord had put his notice in when his wife had run off with a customer. We had the interview and had been successful, Jack's plan had worked, the two officials had only wanted to talk to me. They remarked, 'We know that your wife wants the pub, and why, so we'll aim our questions at you David.'

On the way home we called in at 1 Moorhouse Avenue. 'Mam. Dad. We've got the pub!'

Dad was overjoyed. 'Just remember this,' he went on to say, 'It's a man's right to spend his pound wherever he wants, just be grateful if he spends one in your pub. Oh, and don't iver close Boxing Day.'

I dropped Mavis off and thought I'd call in at the Miners and tell the landlord Alan the news. As I walked in I bumped into two dray men one of which I knew, Cliff Furness. 'Hello Dave, have you heard? Alan's rescinded his notice, posted the letter off today, he's just told us down in the cellar.'

'Oh, good,' I managed. I'll have a pint. I thought, 'See if he tells me, he knows I've applied for it but he won't know I've been given it.'

Alan came up from the cellar, he was surprised to see me. 'Hey up Dave,' he greeted me. 'What'll you have?'

'Pint please Alan.'

'Have you heard anything yet?' He asked.

'No, nothing.' I replied, 'Have you?'

'No, nothing.'

My suspicions were correct. If someone else got the Ship and he rescinded his notice, then David and Mavis will be left high and dry. I immediately went over to the payphone. 'Mavis, ring the brewery and tell them we have changed our minds. We want the Ship, it's a better building, bigger with more potential and has an inside gents toilet which the Miners doesn't. Have you got that? Then ring me back at the Miners OK?'

10 minutes later Mavis rang back. 'We have an interview tomorrow at 10 am.' I had another pint and then left for home.

We got the Ship and moved in a month later on September 13th 1971. I remembered what dad had said.

Six months after that Alan left the Miners, it closed down and never opened its doors again. We went on to run the Ship until April 1st 1985, 14 glorious years. But that's another story.

8. The Breathalyser (1)

Around 1970 the government brought in the dreaded breathalyser. Concern over increased drink related accidents had prompted drastic action. I personally have and always will be in favour of this, having been in the pub trade 30 years, I have seen the positive way that the majority of customers have responded. For myself I never realised the way it would change my life.

Mavis and I had taken the Ship, I was 27 and it was a real shock to the system. I had been used to going out every Saturday night with Mavis and sometimes a midweek trip to the cinema, now I was working every night plus playing rugby.

It soon evolved that Mondays would be my day off, no training to interfere with my day. The pub was quiet Monday lunch times so it seemed natural to take the money to the bank in the morning, join my pub team at night for darts & dominoes, then on to a nightclub later.

After leaving the bank in Wakefield I'd make straight for the Black Rock this was the meeting point for anyone and everyone, especially for those knocking Monday off work, usually miners or those in the building trade.

This particular Monday I had gone out with two pals, Melvyn and Maz. Maz had agreed to drive, he wasn't a big drinker so he was on halves, Mel and I had a session on Guinness in the afternoon in town then on to the Drum and Monkey in Outwood. They had a 4 pm licence whereas town was 3.

After the Drum it was back into town to the Ratcliffe Club who opened at 4.30 pm. From the club it was on to our games night, of course by this time we were slightly inebriated and from the games it was down to the nightclub.

During this mammoth session Maz had chauffeured us all day but he had been on soft drinks most of the time. I came back from the gents, 'Where's Maz?' I asked Melvyn.

'Gone home,' came the reply. 'He's given me the car keys.' he held them in front of me.

I took them from him, 'They're no good to you, you can't drive, c'mon I'll take us home, I'm fine.'

Needless to say it was a dumb decision. About a couple of miles into our journey, flashing lights, 'pull over,' I turned to Melvyn, 'Keep quiet, let me do the talking,' I demanded.

My car door opened and the voice was very precise, 'Please get out of the car, you're under arrest.'

He escorted me to and helped me into the police car which immediately turned around and headed back into Wakefield whereupon I remember walking through the double doors of Wood Street Police Station. To my amazement sat behind the desk was Dick Lowe, second row forward with Dewsbury. We knew each other well and I proceeded to take what I thought was the initiative.

'Now then Dick, where's this white line I'm supposed to walk down?'

'It's Sergeant Lowe to you David and we don't use a white line these days, you can opt for a blood or a urine sample. Which will it be?'

'It might as well be urine, I'm busting anyway.' I joked.

The court case came along and my brief stood up after hearing the police evidence. 'My client offers his sincere apologies mi Lud.'

Fuckin 100 quid he'd charged, I could have stood up and done that and saved some brass. I'd told him about all the mitigating circumstances, having a chauffeur all day etc. etc. A 12 month ban and £200 fine was the magistrate's decision, quite right too but I always maintain I could have walked the white line had there been one.

I paid the fine, did the 12 months and never once weakened, 12 months to the day before I got behind the wheel again. December 17th 1971, pulled over then March 12th 1972, banned. March 12th 1973, back on the road. Our Malc was soon to take advantage of me being mobile again.

It was a lovely summer Sunday, we had been licensees of the Ship Inn for about 18 months, evening trade was healthy but day times were quiet, I was getting a bit bored.

This particular Sunday lunch time our Malc and I were having a pint when he told me, 'I'm doing a job over at Phil's this week.'

'Oh yeah, what's that?' Phil was our brother-in-law, married to our sister Irene, they lived in Bramham, a very well to do area.

'I'm breaking the concrete yard up, carting it away and landscaping the garden. I've asked dad to give me a hand so if you can fit Tuesday and Wednesday in with dad it'll help me out because I'm on another job then,' he continued.

'OK I'll make one in, no problem, what will I be doing?'

'I'll break up concrete on Monday, you and dad can load it onto wagons on Tuesday and Wednesday, then I'll come back an finish the job on Thursday and Friday. Job's a good un. 80 quid in cash for your pocket.'

'Easy,' I declared. 'It'll do me good, a bit of graft.'

Tuesday morning came, I picked dad up from Moorhouse and we arrived in Bramham at about 8.15. The wagon was waiting and so was the concrete, dad gave me a shovel and we proceeded with the loading. Dad was retired from the pit and had been on a light job for a few years before that because of angina. I was a bit concerned about him.

After a few minutes of picking up the big pieces of concrete and throwing them onto the wagon then shovelling the small rubble on, dad decided that I needed to be given a lesson on the best way to use a shovel for this kind of loading, I duly listened and adapted accordingly and I must admit it seemed easier.

The wagons kept rolling in as the hours ticked by, 12 o'clock came. 'Dinner time, ah David,' dad informed me as he moved to walk across to the pub. I thought, 'I'll have some of that.'

Dad opened the door, the landlord looked horrified. 'You can't come...'

'We'll just have two pints of shandy outside, if you don't mind landlord,' dad cut him short.

He brought them to us and accepted the money. 'Working local are you lads?' he asked.

'Just across the road for my son-in-law,' answered dad.

'Oh, who's that?' he enquired.

'Philip, Philip Sykes.'

'Oh my goodness you're Irene's father, do come in, please.'

'Thank you but no,' replied dad. 'When I'm dressed more appropriately I'll be glad to, but I'll not impose on your hospitality.' Dad drank off and bid him good day, I followed suit.

We started shovelling again, half an hour later I was beginning to wish I was still in the pub, any pub. Dad was like a machine, never letting up. I thought, God what was he like 30 years ago. 4 o'clock came and the wagon driver's words, 'Won't get back for any more today, the tip shuts at 4.30.' were music to my ears. Irene had made us a cup of tea at 3 and that 10 minutes was the only break we'd had all afternoon.

I wearily climbed into the car and drove home. It was then that I realised I was training that evening at Bramley.

I told Mavis that I'd take my clothes in a holdall, no point in getting washed and changed twice. I drove over to Bramley at 6.15 with my training gear on looking like something off a jar of jam. At 7 o'clock the coach shouted, 'Let's do a couple of warm up laps lads.'

The first lap was fine then suddenly I felt a new sensation in my body, my mind was fine but my limbs just weren't responding, the harder I tried the slower I went, it was as if I was being held by an invisible force, it was surreal. I watched horrified as I was left hopelessly behind by the others.

'What's up Sammy?' asked our conditioner.

'Don't know,' I replied. 'There's nothing working, can I see the doc?'

'Yeah cummon, I'll take you in.'

When I got inside I was perfectly coherent but my body would not go. The Doctor gave me a pint glass of cold water. 'No training for you my lad,' he informed me. 'Fatigue and dehydration, take two of these now and two before bed, no alcohol tonight and get someone to drive you home later. For now have a hot soak.'

It was the best bath I have ever had in my life. Then the lads got in from their session, 'What the fucks up with you, skiving so and so?'

That I could take, no problem, what was hard to swallow was on arriving back at the Ship, stood in his usual corner chatting to our kid, pint in hand was dad. 'Oh hell,' I thought, I told them what had happened, Malc laughed, dad was concerned. 'Tek notice of what Doctor said and tha should be OK for tomorrow.' I wasn't. I failed. I ached so badly and was so stiff everywhere, Malc had to go with dad. I went to Leeds baths for a sauna and a massage.

Years ago men worked down the pit then came up to play rugby. We don't appreciate this when comparing eras of rugby and making analogies of hard physical fitness training. My contention is that the toughness of the mind and body was by repetitive hard work and tough occupations that the people of the past had to endure, then it's no wonder that we haven't won the ashes since the 70's, before the mines and factories started to close.

When we took on the Aussies we had big, mobile, hard, uncompromising forwards who had inherited the innate toughness needed, through sheer hard work. They had learned the discipline of a fair day's work, no quarter asked or given. If you take a good look at the modern English game, few star players have endured life like their forebears. Training for training's sake, from the age of 17 or 18, honing their bodies but neglecting that which comes with unrelenting hard graft.

I'm not suggesting that every budding athlete must do 10 years on the coal face but it's worth a look at by our so called fitness gurus, that there is more to the athlete's make up than factored stamina, drug enhanced muscle bulk and psychologists telling them how tough they must be. Toughness is inherent, both mentally and physically, honed in the correct manner then polished. The end product will have a chance against anyone, at any sport in which he may show potential.

9. Plate Swallowing is Dangerous

It is suggested that your past flashes through your mind when facing death, well maybe I am lucky. I once travelled that path but didn't complete the journey.

It was a summer lunchtime during the early 1970's. I was in the Ship Inn having a drink with the lads, my two brothers Malc and Brian, Jack Austin made up the drinking school. Joking amongst each other the atmosphere was jovial, noisy and the beer had started to flow. I had developed a bad habit of dropping my false plate in my mouth on regular occasions. It had come loose over the years and I had promised myself to visit the dentist and have it adjusted, but had not got round to it. The reason for the plate was two teeth knocked out against Wakefield by Matt McClouds forearm, he'd apologised immediately so I suppose it was all right.

Well it went like this I had dropped the plate from my upper jaw at the exact time of Jack Austin's punch line, plus it coincided with a deep breath and serious trouble ensured.

I half stood up and tried to breathe. Nothing! Gasping I clutched my throat looked at my brother Brian and I pointed to my mouth as I sank onto my knee's. It was my good fortune that Brian was there he too had a plate fitted and he recognised my predicament and acted accordingly.

'Malc, Jack, tip him up he's choking.'

Brian slapped me several times in the middle of the back, nothing! I could feel myself losing consciousness I could see myself on the river as a boy, on the raft I had made from an old sleeper. I saw girl's faces, I saw my gran's blackberry and apple pie's, my head felt as if it was going to burst, when a sudden thump in the middle of my back made me cough, out came the plate and a bit of bile.

My legs were lowered and I was on my knee's sucking air for dear life. I rose to my feet amidst cheers from the whole room, little did they know what journey I had just been on. I made my excuses and retired upstairs and lay flat out on the bed, my head was throbbing it felt twice its normal size.

Just then the bedroom door opened, it was dad he had seen what had happened.

'Are we all right ah David?'

'Yes dad I'll be back down soon.'

I'd had a real scare I was a split second from being unconscious. If I had gone would I have vomited? One thing for sure I can confirm your past does flash back and it is surreal. Apparently it was Jack who had given me that thump and he always maintained he enjoyed it and I'll always be grateful.

10. Making History

During the season 1973 to 74, Bramley, or the villagers, as they were known, had undoubtedly the best season in their history. We had a new first team coach in Arthur Keegan and no disrespect to our previous coaches but Arthur was someone we could readily identify with. Keith Holiday, our last coach, had achieved a great deal and to be honest was the architect who assembled the team but he was not retained to perhaps savour the fruits of his labour, we will never know.

Arthur had joined Bramley having been a player at Hull. He had the pedigree of being an international full back and had been with the 1966 Tourists. His coach and mentor at Hull was Roy Francis and Arthur introduced to training a lot of innovative methods which he must have picked up during his career under Roy.

The pre-season training had been the most enjoyable for me since 1963 at Wakefield. Enthusiasm and competitiveness was tremendous. Arthur expounded a youthful exuberance that belied his age, we all gradually began to feel more confident in our own abilities. Team spirit was high, there was a fresh air of optimism in the camp, players had a common bond. Most were rejects from previous top-flight teams but Arthur had driven the inferiority complex from everyone. 'You have the talent, express it, play with pride for yourselves and your team mates.' Combined with a maturity that comes with experience and age he mixed the correct formula. Most teams in the league still expected to beat us but we recognised a new undercurrent of respect, so we fed from it. We were like the pack of Hyenas who with commitment and collective team effort could see off the lion at the kill.

The BBC2 Floodlit Trophy had become a much sought after lucrative prize in the sporting calendar, bringing much needed revenue to clubs because progress meant an extra midweek game and prize money at each progressive stage. When the draw was made for the first round, we drew Wakefield Trinity away, we were delighted. Myself, Jack Austin and Barney Ward were the only remaining ex

Wakefield players in the team but Johnny Wolford was Wakefield born and bred. This coupled with the fact that Arthur, Dave Briggs, Ken Huxley and Roy Firth were Dewsbury lads, only a stones throw from Belle Vue. The rivalry was intense and the banter in my pub raised a few eyebrows, for all to a man were Trinity fans.

The match was played at a ferocious pace and intensely competitive, no quarter asked or given, indicative by the score 10-9 and only a few minutes to go, when John Wolford dropped a magnificent goal from about 40 metres to make it 10-11 to us. A lead we hung on to for the last few agonising minutes. The press and the Rugby world were in shock, it was a monumental result for the Villagers, but not to us, that's a fact.

We awaited the draw for the next round. Anyone at home was my philosophy but our confidence was severely dented when Castleford at Bramley was announced. 'Classy Cas' as they were affectionately known, were the Floodlit Trophy Kings having already appeared in three finals and being full of quality footballers. Arthur reminded us we were at home and could ask for no more favours. 'We must earn the rest.' Very true, I remember reflecting.

We worked hard in training and agreed we must get in their faces never letting them settle for the whole 80 minutes. I recall Jack Austin, our left wing being especially fired up on this occasion, for this was the club he had gone to on leaving Wakefield and he had then transferred to Bramley for a meagre 350 quid. He had a score to settle. Make no mistake his attitude was infectious to us all.

That particular November night in 1973 our defence was awesome, we restricted Cas to only one goal, a penalty given away by Jack early on. Such was his commitment that he would inspire us all.

'No more kickable penalties,' came the order from Arthur. 'But keep up the intensity.'

We won the game 13-2 provoking the inevitable press comments that our fairy tale would end in the semi-final.

St. Helens at McLaren Field, yes the mighty Saints would slap the wrists of these upstarts. It was likened to David-v-Goliath and again David had been written off. Surely Saints would not underestimate their task and enter the arena over confident.

I still to this day contend that St. Helens held us in high esteem, they were aware of the quality of our team and this was obvious to us by the ferocity of the opening exchanges. If Saints were to be over confident each player would have been waiting for someone else to turn it on, this was not the case. Some people still did not believe that we were capable of holding our own but that day Saints gave us respect and their best shot.

Three scintillating tries, two from Keith Bollon and the other from John Hughes with two goals from Barney Ward were enough to earn us victory by the odd point in 25 shared. We had come of age, the fairy tale was becoming a saga. We were constantly being reminded by all and sundry that, 'Oh yes, its a wonderful achievement but don't you dare to have the audacity to even contemplate winning the final, after all, your director lost the toss over the telephone for ground advantage.'

We were to travel to meet the powerful Widnes in the final. Like the semi win against Saints, it would be played in daylight, on a Tuesday afternoon because of the power strikes.

We became even bigger outsiders after visiting Widnes before the final and being beaten 27 points to 6 in the league. That setback only served to spur us on, we learned from it and Arthur convinced us that we were capable of turning the tables. We agreed Brian Hogan must not be allowed to bully us and lead their pack, we must intimidate him early and put him off his game. We must find the defensive attitude that had seen us through three epic encounters. We knew we had superior ball skills, vision and pace, what we must do is defend and not panic. Arthur had quietly reminded us of all these points. He left no stone unturned in our preparation and we believed him when he announced, 'I think we will win this game if you have the same confidence in yourselves and belief in your destiny that I do, and that must be to a man, for if we have a chink in our armour Widnes will find it.'

The game was my first cup final as a professional and every bit as exciting and demanding as I expected.

Our team for the record was:

		Previous clubs.
Full Back	Arthur Keegan	Hull F C
Right Wing	Jack Austin	Wakefield - Cas
Right Centre	John Hughes	Market District Leeds*
Left Centre	Keith Bollon	Bramley R U
Left Wing	Peter Goodchild	Doncaster - Halifax
Stand Off	Trevor Briggs	Leeds
Scrum Half	Barney Ward	Wakefield
Prop	David Briggs	Halifax
Hooker	Roy Firth	Hull
Prop	Tony Cheshire	Bradford Northern
2nd Row	David Sampson	Wakefield
2nd Row	Graham Idle	Market District Leeds*
Loose Forward	John Wolford	Balne Lane Wakefield*

Subs
Back	Kenny Huxley	Hull
Forward	Dennis Ashman	Juniors

*Juniors

We got stuck into Brian Hogan as ordered, indeed I gave away the first penalty duly converted, in the opening exchanges but Brian was fully aware we were not taking prisoners. Jack Austin scored in the corner early, to give us a lead we were never to lose, Barney kicked the goal from touch before leaving the field injured. Widnes kicked another penalty, it was nip and tuck, Doug Laughton was having a rare old tussle with Graham Idle, likewise Dave Briggs with Hogan. Our defence held firm, sometimes only by inches but we were confident. Roy Firth requested that I move to prop and Tony Cheshire to 2nd Row. Roy claimed that the reason we had won so little ball was Tony's fault. True to form, all hookers either blame the referee, the scrum half or their props, never themselves. I agreed, it was no big deal to me.

The second half was end to end and as time ticked on we were the ones showing more resolve. Johnny Wolford and myself began to spread the ball wide. Arthur was constantly linking in from full back. Roy was giving us more ball possession from the scrums. Our pressure finally paid off, pace and a sweet passing movement between Trevor Briggs, Keith Bollon and Ken Huxley released Jack Austin down the left. Doug Laughton caught Jack who quickly played the ball. I screamed for it at first receiver, one dummy later I was in, a try without a hand laid on me, a dream come true. Johnny converted and we had some significant daylight between us but Widnes hadn't read the script. A penalty after one bout of pressure and they were back within striking distance, a try and a goal would win it for them. A penalty from John Wolford sent our loyal fans ecstatic but it was not over yet. Back came Widnes, wave after wave, Arthur's voice and example keeping our weary limbs inspired. Then suddenly all the adrenaline came back as we rushed up field to support Peter Goodchild. He had hacked on a loose ball and was scorching toward the Widnes line, it seemed everyone on the field was chasing him, it was all in vain, nobody caught Peter from behind, his aged legs took him all the way but he was obstructed. Try ruled Mr Kershaw. Our fans were enraptured.

That took the score to 7-15, it was game over a few minutes later.

The history of Bramley's epic journey would live forever in the memory of all those who shared the trip and rightly basked in the December sunshine that memorable afternoon, for it mattered little that none of us had tickets for the BBC2 reception marquee.

After bathing our aching bodies it appeared all the tickets had been allocated to the Widnes team in anticipation of their victory. Doug Laughton offered me his ticket, I respectfully declined for I could not and would not allow such a bungling insult by the BBC to come between myself and my team mates. We elected to jump on the bus and watch the match back at the clubhouse. It was truly a day to savour and a night to remember. I had trekked a long journey for a brief stay in Shangri-la. I hope others did too.

11. The Breathalyser (2)

I was driving back from training at Bramley. The day before we had beaten Widnes in the BBC2 Floodlit Trophy Cup Final, we had celebrated into the early hours, Bramley's first major cup in their 95 year history. Training that night had consisted of a hot bath and a couple of bottles of Guinness in the clubhouse, then straight back home to the Ship Inn, or so I thought.

I turned onto Sharp Lane in Middleton, Leeds and about 60 yards on I saw a flashing light being waved about in front of me. I pulled up and low and behold out of the haze came a bobby with a torch. I wound down my window. 'What's the problem officer?' I enquired.

'The problem sir is that you were going a bit fast, don't you think?'

I was a bit taken aback by this and was about to say that if I was going that fast I'd have run over him, but I thought better of it. Play it cool David, humour him, he's only a young rookie out on the beat and he's on his own. 'Sorry officer, just trying to get home.' I thought he'd probably slap my wrist and send me on my way, but no.

First question. 'Where's home?'

I answered. 'Oh, a publican eh?'

Second question. 'And where have you been?'

I answered. 'Oh, a rugby player eh?'

Third question. 'And who do you play for?'

I answered. 'Oh, Bramley eh? They had a good win yesterday, I bet you had a good old celebration eh?'

Fourth question. 'So if you've only had a couple of Guinness's, then you'll have no objection to taking a breath test will you sir?'

Four fuckin questions and I was stymied.

'And I suppose you want me to give you a lift to the fuckin station,' was my angry reply.

'No sir, just get out of the car.' He then spoke into his walkie-talkie, 'Suspect apprehended, please give assistance. Over.'

10 seconds later a Police van came around the corner, I could not believe what was happening. 'Just breathe into this will you sir,' instructed officer 2. I did as asked, convinced that I would be okay

but no I was just over. Number 2 whispered to Number 1, 'He's only just, let him go with a warning.' Yes! I thought, but oh no, PC Plod the brave bastard who had stepped in front of a speeding car armed with only a torch insisted that it was his pull and I had to go to the police station to take either a blood or urine test. I thought, 'Right, last time I took a urine test this time I'll have the blood test, it will take at least an hour to get a doctor in and I might be clear by then.' But guess what? I arrived at the police station in the van to find that the doctor was sat waiting for me, they had radioed in whilst I was locking my car up, in Middleton of all places. I thought to myself, 'I bet it's not there when I get back.'

The blood test came back positive and sure enough I got my court date in Leeds. I'd been to see Ronnie Teeman a Leeds solicitor who was at that time trying to get on the board at Bramley. He had promised me that he would not just get up and apologise for me, also John Hughes, a co-player of mine, had told me that Ronnie had done him a brief and only charged him a couple of bottles of whisky. I thought, 'He's the man for me.'

I turned up on February 6th, 1974 and stood on the court steps awaiting Ronnie, when who came sidling up but the apprehending officer himself PC (Number 1) Plod. 'What does he want?' I thought.

'Mr Sampson,' he uttered. 'Can you just confirm you are he and that this is your correct address?'

Most people reading this will realise I was not very chuffed about this man and will realise why my answer was 'No I won't, FUCK OFF!' He was very shocked.

Just then Ronnie turned up, 'Hi Dave, you ready? We're on first 10 o'clock on the dot. Who's this?' he asked.

'He's the arresting officer,' I replied.

Ronnie turned to the officer, 'What do you want? You're not allowed to approach my client, please go away.'

Same message as I gave him, just phrased differently, that's all.

In court this fearless brave young officer started to address the magistrates. 'Mr Sampson is a resident of the Ship Inn, Lee Moor

Road, Stanley, your worships and does not hold a firearms licence or shotgun certificate...'

'Your Honour,' cried out Ronnie. 'My apologies for interrupting, but is this not a traffic offence before you, what is the relevance as to whether my client has a firearms licence or not?'

'Thank you Mr Teeman,' answered the magistrate. 'Please strike that from the record, unless that is, you intend to offer evidence that a firearm was used or was found on Mr Sampson.'

'No sir, your honour,' spluttered Plod. 'I'm just making the point.'

'Mr Teeman, does your client own a firearm?' asked the magistrate.

'Certainly not your honour,' he replied. Which was the truth, I had given my beloved Canadian Cooy to our Malc before I took the pub.

'Then officer,' snapped the magistrate. 'Kindly keep your statement relevant to the case.'

They'd tear him to pieces of he cocks up again, I thought. PC Plod finished his statement and left the dock, as he did so Ronnie leaned over to me and hissed, 'David, whisper in my ear for about 10 seconds.'

I hadn't a clue why he wanted me to do this but we were on his pitch, playing his game and I was already impressed by this dapper little Jew so I grabbed his arm and whispered, 'Mary had a little lamb...'

Ronnie immediately turned to the magistrate. 'Begging your pardon your worship but my client has just instructed me that the prosecution have failed to note to the court, a previous conviction registered against my client in Wakefield Magistrates Court on March 12th, 1972 and he wishes the court to be aware of this fact. Could your worship ask the prosecution if they are aware?'

'Officer, are you aware of this?' the magistrate asked Plod.

'No your worship,' came the reply.

'Both parties approach the bench,' instructed the magistrate.

It was going my way I thought. The result was that the magistrate turned to me and stated, 'Mr Sampson, the court thanks you for your honesty, Mr Teeman acknowledges that you plead guilty but despite the prosecution's bungling, I have no alternative but to give you the designated sentence of a three year ban. I shall only impose the minimum fine allowed by law of £200 and would like it to go on record that I am far from happy about this case, your arrest and the appalling way the case has been presented by the prosecution.'

Ronnie and I left court and went for a drink and some lunch. 'I'll get you your licence back after two years,' Ronnie claimed. 'Make sure you ring me then.'

'What about payment?' I asked him as we left.

'Oh, I'll send it on. See you later.'

Two days after I received his bill for £250, so much for two bottles of whisky. I remembered he had quizzed me about the pub and how it was doing whilst we ate lunch that day, maybe if I had told him I was skint it might have been different but I'd done the crime now I had to do the time. The taxi drivers in Wakefield would be rubbing their hands.

The two years passed and sure enough I contacted Ronnie. 'OK David, I'll apply for a court date.' he told me. It was February 1976 and Ronnie wrote and told me we'd been given a hearing on the 10th of May.

'We'll have to have a strong application,' he informed me at my briefing.

I was still running the pub and playing rugby for Bramley but I had also started up a building business during the day with my brother Malcolm, only I had to have a chauffeur, this job was Mel Castle's, my mate who had been in the car with me on that first fateful occasion.

I informed Ronnie that I employed around 14 people on the building job, a dozen in the pub plus the chauffeur, the cost of which might possibly break me. If I couldn't get back driving myself soon then look how many people could loose their jobs.

'Add that to the magistrate's comments at your trial,' Ronnie reminded me 'And that's it, that's our plan of attack.'

The court case came around and Ronnie was as sharp as a razor, he had to be, the opposition from the prosecution was intense, they had even brought a big wheel over from Wakefield to oppose my application. 'Three years should mean three years,' they stated. 'It's the deterrent we demand. There has never been anyone who has had their ban removed from three years to less since it was introduced.'

'But there are many mitigating circumstances relevant in this case,' argued Ronnie.

When the magistrates came back into the room I thought to myself, 'Ah well if I lose it's only another nine months.' I had not driven once during the two years and three months that had passed, I was on first name terms with so many taxi drivers I'd lost count. The magistrate's comments were sweet music to my ears, I was the first in Leeds to beat the three year ban. I drove the car home and told Mel 'Right mate you're back on the tools full time.' Mel was actually a brickie and he went on to work for many years with our kid.

That night back at the pub we celebrated, I was the DJ playing the music and drinking my beloved Holsten Pils, in those days we would celebrate the dog's birthday given half a chance. One thing I told myself after that court case was 'I'm not going down that road again.'

12. The Inevitable

If we liken our bodies to say a car then there are many parallels, if you put cheap oil and petrol in you will get substandard performances and a less reliable vehicle. If you drive in the fast lane from A to B all the time every time, you will lessen its life expectancy and that applies pro-rata be it a Rolls Royce or a Mini. Regular servicing may help extend its life but parts will have to be changed more often.

If you're a sportsman the international's and Olympian's can be likened to the Rolls the clubmen the Mini all in good nick when new but some when they start deteriorating go down the slope quicker than others dependent on how they have been looked after, or more to the point looked after themselves. In my case, I believe I was a car in the mid range a Ford Cortina or Vauxhall maybe. I looked after myself in the early years then pushed to the limit until I was only fit for a short journey on a Sunday afternoon then put back in the garage for a weeks rest. My cheap oil was the brandy my petrol the beer, the fast lane was bed by 3 am instead of 10 pm. My servicing was intermittent rather than regular and not always by qualified mechanics.

It was time to stop drinking one doc said, forever! Another opinion was sought, he compromised. 'Let's work at it steadily, there are no spare parts available so we will have to make this one work for as long as possible, that's if you want to see your grandchildren grow up.'

The part in question my liver was spluttering to an inevitable halt. If I'd carried on abusing it, well it's now 2001, I have two grandchildren seven and four so the compromise appears to be working. After rugby as each year goes by I slow down a little more, but in doing so I've learned to appreciate time differently and enjoy it. The number of days are diminishing, I'm on the hard shoulder rather than the fast lane but I take heart that another trip to Shangri-la is just around the corner. In fact picking a 'dream team' would be a visit to Shangri-la for some hardened fans. It was for me too. Having watched, played with and against and coached I have tried to be constructive in choice bearing in mind the modernisation of the game. Only Great Britain players are eligible.

We all often fantasize about picking our dream teams well these are Dave Sampson's two dream teams from 1956 to 2001.

Probables V Possibles

1.	Paul Charlton (Salford)	Lewis Jones (Leeds)
2.	Berywn Jones (Wakefield)	Billy Boston (Wigan)
3.	Ellery Hanley (Bfd/Wigan)	Paul Newlove (Leeds)
4.	Keith Holden (Wigan)	Neil Fox (Wakefield)
5.	Mick Sullivan (Hudd/Wigan)	Martin Offiah (Wigan)
6.	John Joyner (Cas)	Alan Hardisty (Cas/Leeds)
7.	Alex Murphy (St Helens)	Roger Millward (Cas/Leeds)
8.	Kevin Ward (Cas/Manley)	Dennis Hartley (Cas/Hunslet)
9.	Tony Fisher (Bfd/Cas/Leeds)	Keiron Cunningham (Wigan)
10.	Cliff Watson (St Helens)	Lee Crooks (Hull/Leeds/Cas)
11.	Phil Lowe (HKR)	Dick Huddart (St Helens)
12.	Jim Thompson (Feth/Bfd)	George Nichols (Widnes/St Helens)
13.	Derek Turner (Wakefield)	Mal Reilly (Cas)
14.	Kris Radlinski (Wigan)	Jason Robinson (HKR)
15.	Dick Gemmel (Leeds/Hull)	Joe Lydon (Wigan)
16.	Doug Laughton (Widnes)	Len Casey (HKR)
17.	Vince Karalius (Widnes)	Dennis Betts (Wigan)
	Coach: Bev Risman	Coach: Roy Francis
	Ass Coach: Phil Larder	Ass Coach: Clive Griffiths

Travelling reserves, Jack Austin and John Woolford, because they never got the recognition they deserved.

I believe either of these two teams would win any ashes series against a similarly compiled Australian tour party and one thing I also believe that the absence of so many modern day players is indicative of the influx of so many foreign imports and its consequential restriction. I have omitted players pre 1956 because I am not qualified to give an opinion and I've not necessarily included all the clubs they played for as space does not permit.

Of the development of our own talent I had the privilege of playing alongside or against most of these players both as a centre and forward. Other people may contend that there are players not included who are more deserving but these are my choices. I am adamant about one thing also if say Keiron Cunningham or Paul Newlove had played in the 60's they would have been stars as they are today. I am also equally adamant that had say Derek Turner or Lewis Jones played today they too would be star players.

When I was a young man I would scoff at the idea that players of yesteryear could have been stars of my era but in the last 45 years I have worn the T-shirt gained the experience and I can only apologise to those gladiators for my being so presumptuous. I believe now we as a nation have collectively been diluted by the progressive improvement of our lifestyle at the cost of many values, skills and disciplines that went together in making us great. I believe we have sold the soul of our game to the dollar.

I feel sure Mr Murdoch and his cronies will not be happy until we have a game that produces regular scores as in basketball say 110-90. It appals me that we have Australian supremo's running the game in England and judging who should get the job, an Aussie or an Englishman. We have lost the likes of Phil Larder, Ellery Hanley, Joe Lydon and Clive Griffiths to Rugby Union. Would the NFL in Australia allow that to happen to the cream of the Australian coaching and admin talent? No is the answer. I will contend that we have learnt an awful lot from the Australians but mark my words they will have gleaned from us but they are too subtle to admit to it.

In addition, they could not cope with the Rodger Millward's and Chuck Hardisty's of our game so it has been systematically changed and will continue to do so to keep them ahead. It's too much one way traffic for my liking, the changes in administration have been so fast and furious of late, that the adage there's no smoke without fire must make one think that all's not well at the top. No other industry or sport in the world would allow a coaching ratio of ninety five percent of the top jobs going to overseas coaches and then justify it to the workforce. And something else, I'll bet Graham Steadman who recently took over at Cas from Stuart Raper will be on less money than Stuart was but if he is to make the job his own he will be expected to do as well as Stuart. It's just that we Brits are more proud to get the job and we sell ourselves short by accepting less.

The only Aussies I've known who come over here have usually been the ambitious ones who want to make a name and then get a top job back home. Well if our lads are going to get offered the jobs, I hope the Boardroom give them their dignity by paying them accordingly the same as the Aussie. I hope people do not assume that I am anti-Aussie. I am not. Stuart Raper has done a wonderful job at Castleford on a tight budget and he has earned my admiration and respect as do many other Australians but in talking to so many ex-players and coaches, I find we are stifling their ambition and confidence. From the top down we need to contract our ageing play-ers into supportive roles and assure them that if they work hard they will have a future. We need to make more money available using the Conference League as a base for our qualified ex-pro's to obtain the experience at ground level but the structured way to the top must be clearly visible for them so they can generate enthusiasm and ambition to go for it.

In turn the Conference nationally will grow and we will be truly a national game played by Englishmen coached by Englishmen and watched by thousands of partisan Englishmen. Only then can we hope to have a say in the global future of our game and compete for world domination.

My worst fears are that if our great game continues to develop into a truly national sport, the amateur and professional coaching structure will be overloaded with Australians. If the game of the future is to be styled by the Aussies we must endeavour now to come forward with a framework for the future for our coaches based on true English values. And the coaches must begin to help themselves for it will not be handed on a silver spoon by some of our sanctimonious prejudiced directors for they are the deputies in their hallowed halls looking down on the lad that might make good from down the road. He stands little chance against the glamorous slick tongued overseas applicant unless he too fulfils his thirst for learning, presentation and application as they do. Once given a chance, well then it's up to him but it will be deemed progress and progression. In coaching these are very important words.

I applaud Sir Rodney Walker in his attempts to bring the game under one umbrella for this surely is the way forward and if some people push personal ambitions aside for the sake of the game, then it will be a momentous occasion, a giant stride forward for all.

After naming a probables v possibles I have now compiled a dream team with an analysis. I hope you enjoy the arguments it is bound to cause.

Position 1. Full back
If we take the two full backs Paul Charlton and Lewis Jones, both had superb hands and were safe under a high ball. Both had bags of pace and tremendous vision. Paul Charlton for me still holds the record of most tries in a season with 33 and we cannot accept any Northern Ford Premiership players claiming Paul's record. That to me is unacceptable. Lewis Jones had an excellent boot, both goal kicking and from his hands. He held an edge over Paul, but if I had a kicker in my team Paul would just get the nod, but it's close.

Position 2. Wing
Well, Billy Boston was probably the greatest I ever saw and I did have the privilege of playing against him but he was with Blackpool, not Wigan and clearly past his best. My choice of Berwyn Jones may shock one or two, but he would have given Martin Offiah five yards start and beaten him by five, and that's the truth - he was the fastest ever. He had a good solid defence and was as brave as they come. Wakefield were on the decline a little I suppose when he signed, but he toured in 1966 and scored some glorious tries. Had he played from 1959 to 63 he would be a household name even now.

Position 3. Centre
It is again close, both players have all the qualities needed, pace, good

hands, vision, the lot. But Ellery would get my vote, he like Billy was one of the all time greats.

Position 4. Centre

Here again it's close at left centre, but my vote would go to Neil Fox. He has to rank as one of, if not the greatest of all time. I watched him, played alongside him and against him, and he had it all. Keith Holden on the other hand was also the kind of player every coach would pick before anyone else. Fifteen and a half stone, quick and a fearsome presence. I was glad to see him retire.

Position 5. Wing

The legendary Mick Sullivan or Martin Offiah? Well, it would be Martin just because he had a little more vision and versatility in his game. Along with Billy Boston and Tom Vollenhoven, Martin ranks in the top five wingers of all time.

Position 6. Off half

This is the tricky one, some would argue John Joyner was a better centre, some would argue Rodger Millward was a better stand off than scrum half, others that Alan Hardisty had no peers. Of the three I consider that John Joyner at thirteen and a half stone with pace to burn and hands and vision would have been an ideal number six, and is therefore my choice.

Position 7. Scrum half

This is equally as tricky but Murph gets my vote by a cat's whisker because like Rodger he could be a match winner from nothing but Murph's aggression and ability to drive others gives him the edge.

Position 8. Prop

Kevin Ward gets my vote, not because I was instrumental in him turning his back on soccer, or his signing for Cas, or the fact that he comes from my own village but because he went over to Australia and proved that he was amongst the best ever - and that's from the Aussies!

Position 9. Hooker
Tony Fisher at his best was a fearsome competitor, but it would be Keiron Cunningham because his extra pace and dummy half capabilities would give him the narrowest of edges.

Position 10. Prop
Cliff Watson or Lee Crooks? Well no one can deny that there's little to choose between them. Lee had probably better hands but Cliff gets my vote, just.

Position 11. Second forward
Choosing the second row I have looked for the right blend, a runner and a grafter. Phil Lowe would be my number 11, just. Again close, for Dick Huddart was an awesome runner.

Position 12. Second forward
I go for Jim Thompson. His high work rate and fearless approach just gave him the edge over George Nichols who had few equals. Dennis Betts is a great forward as was Doug Laughton, but I make no apologies for omitting them.

Position 13. Loose forward
Derek Turner was the more direct of the two and like Mal Reilly earned an awesome reputation from the Aussies. Derek had superb hands and an intelligent boot, neither would take a backward step. I was privileged that as a nineteen year old I played with Derek, when like Billy Boston, he was probably past his best and with Mal at Cas when he too would admit his best days had been in Australia. However, Mal gets my vote because his phenomenal work rate and fitness were unsurpassed. I know, I trained with them both.

In choosing the subs for my dream team I have considered all players from both squads, including those omitted at first choice.

14. Jason Robinson for his explosive running and utility value at full back, wing and half back.

15. Rodger Millward with his utility and ability to score from broken play would make him a match breaker.

16. Lee Crooks could play prop or second row and had great vision.

17. Derek Turner, inspirational, would give any side a lift when coming off the bench.

My all time dream team

1. Paul Charlton
2. Billy Boston
3. Ellery Hanley
4. Neil Fox
5. Martin Offiah
6. John Joyner
7. Alex Murphy
8. Kevin Ward
9. Keiron Cunningham
10. Cliff Watson
11. Phil Lowe
12. Jimmy Thompson
13. Malcolm Reilly
14. Jason Robinson
15. Rodger Millward
16. Lee Crooks
17. Derek Turner

Coach. Roy Francis. Hull. A visionary man who would command respect from such an illustrious array of talent.

Assistant Coach. Clive Griffiths. He's earned it doing what he's done with Wales.

Physio. Paddy Armour, Wakefield Trinity. The governor of all time.

Oily rubber downers. Stuart Griss Ansell (he's my mate!). Dave Sampson (it's my team!)

Kit men. Jack Austin. Too many clubs to list. John Woolford of Bramley and Bradford Northern (so we could reminisce and have a drink after).

Bus driver. Roy Firth, Hull and Bramley. He would never fall asleep at the wheel - he never did in bed!

13. The Making of Harry's Day

Hundreds of pubs throughout the country would have their pub trips, some to the races, some to Wembley. We at the Ship were no different, the racing trip had long been established before my arrival it was just that the numbers increased. Haydock Park, then Blackpool at night, Thirsk then Scarborough or Bridlington.

They were rowdy fun filled days normally free from trouble, mixed ages from 18 to 80 all consuming alcohol to their maximum. One such trip to Haydock then Warrington Rugby League Social Club had been a particularly good day, alas on the bus journey home, an altercation between two customers exploded into blows being exchanged. Our kid and myself quelled the initial protagonists but only for a few miles. Next I knew Ray had struck Ernie with a full bottle splitting his head rather badly, blood was running from his hairline onto his face. Ernie was an ex boxer, 'International amateur and top pro,' he'd calmly announced to our kid.

'I don't think there was any need for that, do you Malc?'

'No Ernie it was out of order.'

Ray had sat down again but he was beginning to sober up, I think he was more shocked that it hadn't caused more damage or had the desired effect. Ernie's reaction was to lean over and drop a short right on Ray's chin, which then initiated a response from Ted whose short flurry of punches had no effect whatsoever. A short left from Ernie sat Ted back in his seat, his and Ray's heads were now serenely propping each other up. Malc was holding Ernie by now and I was holding Larry back. 'Larry it's not your problem keep out of it.' I pleaded, 'He's out of your league.' But Larry was Larry, one of the rare breed of miners who actually played rugby union for Rodillians our local team. Malc and myself kept them apart until the bus came to a halt outside the Ship. I woke Ted and Ray, they had slept peacefully ever since Ernie clipped them both. Everyone was rushing to get off climbing over the stacks of beer crates in the isles, not wanting to miss the action for Larry had constantly challenged Ernie.

'As soon as the bus stops.' Larry goaded.

'Whenever.' was Ernie's reply.

Malc escorted Ernie into the car park of the Miners, a boarded up derelict old pub that had seen many a tussle in years gone by. I had deliberately kept Larry back and apart from the driver we were the last off the bus. The arena was now formed, a full circle of eager inebriated mates were now divided, each unconsciously taking sides and shouting encouragement. I pleaded one last time, 'Shake hands and we can all go home,' but to no avail. Both protagonists circled the inner perimeter, Ernie shuffled into the centre, Larry went up onto his toes and one jab, two jabs. Ernie simply blinked, he was stalking Larry trying to cut him off. I was surprised at Larry two more jabs and a right cross, which must have reopened Ernie's cut because blood was now flowing down his forehead and over either side of the bridge of his nose. Ernie kept the pressure on Larry but it was Larry on points so far however Larry was visibly tiring. The crowd were unconsciously closing the size of the arena and coupled with the beer consumed and the unevenness of the ground, the exchanges were fiercer and closer. Ernie was landing the heavier shots, one to Larry's rib cage, he went down on one knee. 'Have you had enough?' puffed Ernie. Larry took a deep breath and rose up lunging in the same instance at Ernie only to be the recipient of a left hook that downed him again. But this time Ernie pounced atop Larry, straddling his stomach he brought his head down on Larry's nose. 'Have you had enough?'

'Fuck off!' spluttered Larry through his now bleeding swollen lips.

Our Malc and I simultaneously moved forward. 'Enough's, enough lads everybody's going home,' we parted them our Malc disappearing with Ernie, I took Larry into the pub toilets, he cleaned up and I loaned him a sweater to go home in. A couple of the lads helped me off load the empties. We decided to join Harry Willy Firth in the beer garden, it was 4 am. 'Might as well finish last few bottles David?'

'Yes OK Harry.'

Harry was in his late 60's one of nine brothers, he too a former miner. 'I'm sorry it had to end like that,' I quipped to Harry as I sank onto my plastic chair.

'Nah don't bi sorry David, a bit of excitement made day for me.

Larry had gained a lot of people's respect I had noted.

I opened the doors 11.55 Sunday morning, first two customers Ernie and Larry, I bought the first two pints. They drank together all Sunday lunch and many times after that.

On reporting to dad about this epic encounter, he had replied, 'I wish I'd a pound for every time Ernie's dad Harry had fought on Miner's car park. He was a hard man and a good collier.'

14. Ding Dong Dell

A windy, cold Christmas storm was blowing across Lee Moor, it was a couple of nights before Christmas Eve but it wasn't a Christmas I was looking forward to. My trusty old Labrador, Dell, had gone missing, he was blind but had a keen nose and invariably got about without much trouble but suddenly it was as if he had just been whisked away, no one had seen him. This particular night I couldn't sleep, there was something in the wind that didn't quite sound right. Dell was a dog that never ever barked, strange, you might think, but true. From the day we moved into the Ship, no one had ever heard Dell bark. For the first six years of his life he had lived in a pen with Rex, our Malc's dog, but when we took the Ship, I moved him in. I think he was so comfortable with moving indoors that he decided not to bark again.

During the night I opened my bedroom window and was positive I could hear a distinct howl from an animal, it must be Dell I reasoned. I quickly dressed and walked out looking in the hedgerows, had he been knocked down and crawled for cover? But there was no cover. It was a bleak December, the wind kept moving and I couldn't pinpoint the howl. It was the same again the following night even after the kids had done a daylight search and shout. Maybe it was the wind playing tricks on my ears.

Christmas Eve came and went, as did Christmas Day. Dell had been a part of the family since 1965 and the pub since 1971. It was now 1973. I was sure I could hear him again and stood out front giving a soft whistle hoping to spark a response. The old pub, the Miners Arms, across the road had been demolished leaving it rubble strewn with some areas of short grass. I walked over it, but nothing, the sounds had once again gone silent, I went back in.

Boxing Day was always busy and as Dad had told me, I never closed on Boxing Day, we would be packed out all day and that's how it was. Suddenly the front door opened and Barry Stakes, a neighbour, shouted, 'David, I've found Dell!' I rushed out expecting the worst.

My parents George and Leah.

The author aged four.

Left to right, Don Vines, Derek Turner, Malcolm Sampson (with ball), Jack Wilkinson, Terry Clawson. 1960 Challenge Cup semi final Wakefield v Featherstone at Odsal.

Coaching week at Bisham Abbey 1963, the author with the ball.

The Battle of Belle Vue, Wakefield Trinity v Australian Tourists. Malcolm Sampson tries to evade the green wall 1959-60.

Wembley 1963 Challenge Cup final. Malcolm Sampson scores for Wakefield against Wigan.

Wakefield Trinity before an away fixture against Batley 1964-65. Back row left to right, Keith Holliday, Ted Campbell, Malcolm Storey, Harold Poynton, Roy Hawksley, Oupa Coetzer, Willis Rushton. Front row, Malcolm Sampson, Berwyn Jones, Don Vines, Dave Sampson, Bob Haigh, Gerry Round.

Wakefield Trinity squad before the 1965 Challenge Cup semi final against Hunslet. The author front row, second from the right. Malcolm Sampson back row, first left.

Wedding day December 3rd 1966. The author turns out for Bramley v Leeds at Headingley whilst Mavis looks on.

Bramley's Dave Sampson and Jack Austin covering the threat from Brian Jefferson at Keighley, 1970-71.

Denise Ramsden wins the
YWAAA 100 yards at
Castleford.

No quarter asked, none given. The author tackles
Sid Hynes in the Bramley v Leeds derby 1973.

Bramley before beating St Helens in the Floodlit Trophy semi final
1973. Back row left to right, Ken Huxley, Jack Austin, Dave Sampson,
Tony Cheshire, Roy Firth, Graham Idle, Peter Goodchild, David Briggs,
Dennis Ashman. Front row, Harry O'Keefe, John Hughes, Barney Ward,
Keith Bollon, Arthur Keegan, John Wolford, Trevor Briggs.

The Ship Inn.

The author scoring against Widnes in the 1973 Floodlit Trophy final victory.

'Ahoy you scurvy dogs' Sammy's Super Ship.

The author and his father George celebrate victory in the 1972 darts and dominoes championships at the Ship.

Wembley 1986, Castlford victorious in the Challenge Cup final. Jamie Sandy darts for the line.

The final whistle. left to right, Stuart (animal) Walker, Mal Reilly, Dave Sampson.

Assistant coaches John Kear and Dave Sampson celebrate the Challenge Cup victory.

Wembley celebrations Gary Connell, Dennis Tiffany and Dave Sampson.

Castleford A-team after winning the Yorkshire Cup. Dave Sampson (coach) holding trophy.

Parading the Challenge Cup through the streets of Castleford.

Karaoke Kings, left to right, Dave Sampson, Kevin Ward, Colin Scott.

Stanley Rangers 1989. The author back row second from right.

Wembley 1997, Dean Sampson playing for Great Britain against Australia.

Lee Sampson playing for Doncaster launches into a tackle.

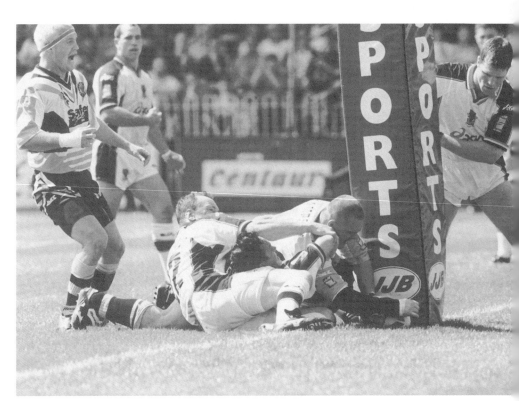

1999, Dean Sampson scores his 50th try against Bradford Bulls.

Castleford Tigers warm weather training in Lanzarote. Dean Sampson in the foreground.

Dean makes his 400th appearance for Castleford Tigers.

Dean Sampson in Castleford Tigers publicity shot.

Scottish Amicable Challenge 2001. Barbarians' Geordan Murphy fends off England's Paul Sampson.

Several family members today at a Samson's party night, left to right Malcolm, Brian, Dave, boxer Ernie Shavers and son's Dean, Lee and Jonathon.

To my absolute amazement Barry had crossed the road and not 10 feet into some sparse grass was a manhole, no lid on, about five feet deep. There laid in the bottom was Dell, he was half looking up with those big glazed green eyes, not seeing but knowing he was going to be rescued from his tomb. Dell was exceptionally big for a Labrador, about 12 stone, but our Malc didn't hesitate for one moment. 'Take a leg each and lower me in.' He gripped Dell's thick fur around his neck and we hauled them both up. Dell stood, shook himself from head to tail and waddled back across to the pub to a rapturous welcome. Everyone had a good drink that day, not that they wouldn't have anyway but Dell's rescue made it a very special day. The manhole was filled in the next day. If Dell had barked I would have found him, I was only six feet away from him on Christmas night, but he didn't, strange?

15. A Day at the Hospital

My appointment was 10 am at Pinderfields Fracture Clinic. I checked in. The girl on reception greeted me. 'Hi David, just a check up is it?'

'Yes love,' I replied. 'And probably a new pot, this one has broken in two.'

'How did that happen?' she enquired.

'I had to eject someone from the pub last night and it broke on his head, listen can you get me dealt with quickly, I have to get back to the pub for opening time?'

'You shouldn't be working with a broken arm.'

'Not in a ideal world my love but if I draw sick the DHSS would hang me if I was seen to do as much as pick up a glass for washing, so I don't draw sick, not worth the trouble.'

'Mr David Sampson.' the voice over the tannoy announced about five minutes later, well done I thought, in and out in 15 minutes flat. I had broken my forearm, both bones clean through the middle. I had gone to tackle Mike Smith, the Featherstone Rovers stand off half, he ducked his head and I hit him across the top of his skull. I knew exactly what I'd done, this was the third time, all self inflicted. No complaints from me, it was not a high shot, he just had this habit of ducking and I had this habit of swinging.

Into the potting shed I went and the two nurses had a good giggle at my pot in two pieces as they began to cut it off. After four weeks in plaster the limb is usually much thinner and obviously weaker but my forearm seemed to be, well, misshapen and my hand was at a sort of twisted angle. I immediately feared the worst and the X-ray confirmed my fear, you didn't need to be an orthopaedic surgeon to know something was wrong. I pinched a look at the films as I walked back down the corridor from the X-ray department, my heart sank, a bleeding month wasted, I had better ring home.

'Mavis, I might not be home for a while, there seems to be a problem with my arm. I'll ring you back once I've seen the specialist.'

'Don't you go out on the booze all day and say you've been at the hospital,' she snapped. 'You know we've got a buffet for Waddington's this afternoon.' She knew me well. By this time I already knew they would have to break the arm again, then reset it.

My worst fears were well founded when the consultant asked whether I'd had anything to eat or drink since 12 o'clock the night before. I felt like saying yes, meat and two veg. but that would only be prolonging things so I answered no. It was about 5 pm when I came around and sat up. I was in a small anteroom, I remember my lips were dry and my arm was throbbing, getting worse by the minute when the nurse came in. 'You can go David, your Mavis is outside waiting in the car.' She had rung to see where I was. I later found out that she had tried the Black Rock first.

'Get me Dr Singh,' I instructed Mavis when we got home. 'This pain is excruciating.'

Doctor Singh was a regular customer and friend, he had helped me out after a car crash I'd had, but that's another story. Sing-a-long, as we affectionately called him, duly arrived and after I explained what had happened he went out to his car and brought in some tablets which I took and then retired to bed, it was about 7 pm. Now this is the strangest part of the story because the pain quickly subsided and I was laid in bed, numb from the neck down, this lasted all night but I couldn't get to sleep. Come the next morning I was so tired I eventually dropped off and didn't wake until 6 pm. I ate my tea, washed, changed and went downstairs into the pub to tell the story which then passed around the village, as a result more people came to see me, I retold my story, we sold more beer, and so on and so on.

The arm finally healed and I played again eight weeks later none the worse but with my own, specially made arm pad of surgical stocking and beer mats, which I wet and moulded onto my forearm, I would always put this on after the touch judge had done his kit inspection. I never broke my forearm again, that fourth time was a lesson learned the hard way.

16. A Good Reason for Seat Belts

I have seemingly had a charmed life compared to some in respect of drinking and driving but I've not always been the driver.

Jack Austin and I decided one night after training at Bramley to have a couple of hours over in our Brian's night club in Shipley, well he was the manager, and I had been shopping that day, brand new tan suede jacket and shoes, beige cavalry twill slacks, cream shirt. We had a couple of hours with Brian, the intention was then to go on to Heppy's in Wakefield.

There was a snowstorm starting as we left Shipley at around 11 pm. Jack was driving, a Morris 1100 I recall. As we drove through Bradford city centre and up the hill onto Wakefield Road, the snow had settled making driving difficult and the windscreen wipers were struggling to keep up. Luckily we were not travelling too fast because Jack suddenly lost control of the car, we mounted the kerb and proceeded to skid toward a lamppost, one of the concrete type. I remember saying to Jack, 'It looks like ours but don't brake! Don't brake!' Jack was a bloody good winger but a crap driver, he braked. We doubled our speed and I went through the windscreen, Jack had held on to the wheel and cushioned his impact, he was unscathed, I didn't know the extent of my injuries but I was alert. The blizzard was blowing into our faces through the broken windscreen and we could see a pub across the road, suddenly a police car pulled up outside the pub but facing the opposite direction to us, the police piled out and into the pub, they were oblivious to us. The lamppost was embedded about two feet into the centre of the car bonnet, I looked to my left, there were some advertisement hoardings and I could see a gap. 'Jack, follow me,' I instructed. We ran and hid for a few minutes, then as we started to walk away down a side street a taxi appeared right in front of us. The driver looked horrified and scared as I stood in the beam of his headlights, both arms raised. It was only now, in the light, that I looked at myself. I was covered in blood, my shirt, tie, coat, trousers, even my shoes. 'Take us to the hospital please, Pinderfields, I don't want to go to Bradford.' Jack had climbed in the back. 'What about the car?' he'd asked.

'Never mind the car, here's what we do. Go back to the Ship, take half a bottle of whisky off the bar shelf, drop me off there and then get this guy to drop you off at home. Make sure you swig some whisky, if the police arrive tell them you had to get me to the hospital first, have you got that mate?'

'Yes.'

'Oh, with Mavis being pregnant you'd better go into the pub first and break the news to her gently, tell her I'm OK.'

'Got you,' Jack replied.

As we pulled up at the Ship I knew I'd lost a lot of blood but I'd looked after Jack. I could ring Doctor Singh, he would make sure I wasn't butchered by casualty when sewing me up and sewing up was what I was going to need, I'd had a look in the drivers mirror and I was cut up pretty badly.

The Ship was in darkness, Mavis must be in bed, I assumed. I sent Jack to the back door, a few minutes later he came out with a bottle of whisky. 'I said half a bottle, you cheeky git,' I joked. 'Do as I told you and I'll see you tomorrow.'

I entered the back door. Mavis nearly fainted. 'What the hell's happened to you?' She shrieked. Mavis was several months gone with our Rebecca.

'Didn't Jack tell you?' I asked.

'He just blurted, 'have you a bottle of whisky?' I gave him one and he went, never said a dickie bird. What's happened?'

'Look I'm OK. Ring Singh-a-long, ask him to come and take me to the hospital please.' Ten minutes later he was with us.

'Got some glass in there I'll bet David, cummon we'd better get you to casualty.'

It was 1 o'clock in the morning and 46 stitches later when I was discharged. On returning home I went to bed and slept until lunch time. My face was a mess, swollen, black, red, blue, eyes like slits, I'd amazed myself thinking about the previous nights events. Jack called in the pub during his dinner hour, he was gob smacked when he saw me and very apologetic. I had to go back to the hospital later for some glass removing from my face but I healed, we made light of it all. The police didn't visit Jack until two days later and he still owes me for the whisky. I got a new outfit from the insurance. Lady luck had been in our corner that night back in 1975.

17. Times Flies

When any player completed 10 years service with one club, inclusive of 250 games, he could apply to the Rugby League for a testimonial, this befell on me at Bramley. I'd had my ups and downs with the club but had always given a hundred and ten percent for them. I had an affinity towards them that comes with any relationship of this length of time.

I had married Mavis just after signing that glorious summer day in July 1966. I had played on my wedding day on December 3rd because they asked me to. This was against Leeds at Headingley. Our Malc also played, my wife Mavis and his wife Avis both attended. I recall Avis mentioning after the match how impressed she was with our ground, she had only ever been to Belle Vue and Wembley before. Our Malc had to break it to her that we were playing away.

Bramley's McLaren Field held special memories for me. I had done all the plumbing and heating in the new stand. We had shared triumph against all odds in winning the Floodlit Trophy away at Widnes. Most of all I had made some lifelong friends along the way, so I was looking forward to a successful testimonial. I put a committee together and a few events were planned. A soccer match against Bradford Variety Club. This was a real fun day and one of the famous Worthington's told me I should have taken up soccer. We all had drinks after and raised a few quid which was put in the bank account that the club had opened. Next up was a charity concert at Bramley Labour Club, I organised a bus full of regulars from my pub in Stanley and told them it was a mystery trip. The entertainment was organised by my old pal Frank McManus, he booked some quality acts who worked for expenses only. The club was heaving and the show was fantastic. The bar staff were pissed, the doormen were pissed, the committee were pissed, everybody, including my bus party was pissed. Steve Butterfield from my party won both bingo cards, £18, he was ecstatic, mind you he was a tight bugger and even happier on the return bus journey when he won a further £9 on the domino card. It was one hell of a Monday night.

At training I asked Ronnie the kit man if he had any idea as to how much we had made. 'Best ask Frank,' he replied. Frank referred me to the committee, 'They're doing the accounts in their room, go see em now before they go.'

I did as advised only to be told, 'Well you see David, it's like this. There were four acts at £20 each, two doormen, raffle tickets, bingo cards, bar staff and you'd said to get the committee a drink. It works out at a total profit to go to the bank, of £9.'

I smiled and walked out. Nine bleeding quid, there were 52 of us from the Ship at a quid apiece, Steve Butterfield got twice as much as me on the bingo. In future I'll organise things, I thought. Nobody's to blame, but everybody's to blame. I'd arranged a couple more functions myself back in Stanley and now had a grand total of £612 in the bank and a committee that had disintegrated.

Peter Fox, our coach had moved to Bradford and was to take John Woolford and Jack Austin, two of my best pals with him. Tommy Smales had taken over as coach, a lovely man but even though I was club captain, I could not motivate myself for the club. 'I will play for the A-team until January 6th, then I'm retiring.' He was very understanding and accepted that we had a young A-team and it would be of benefit to them, it was also of benefit to me.

We won nine games from 11 and I had some cracking players around me, Geoff Tennant and Steve Hunter from Stanley, Roy and Ian Sampson, it was a sad day indeed as I approached my last game in the A-team, Wakefield at Bramley.

As I walked toward the dressing room I noticed a big Jag parked up, I recognised it as belonging to Phil Brunt, the Castleford chairman and wondered what was he doing here? I had a vague idea, just before kick-off Jim Bowden, one of the directors came to me, 'David, have a good un my son.' 'Have a good un?' I thought. 'He's been at the club for six months and never spoken to me before. I know why he wants me to have a good un, well they can get stuffed, they're not making a penny out of me, I've finished as of today and I'm going to have a good un because that's what I'd intended anyway.'

Everything that could go right when you're spraying passes, dummies, drop goals, bursts, off loads, went right for me that day. I announced to the lads after the match that it had been my last game, wished them all the best for the future then headed for the bar. Doug Alton, the chairman barred my way. 'David, there's someone I'd like you to meet, can you come into the boardroom?' Well, I don't like to appear rude so I went along with it. Now anyone who knew Phil Brunt the Cas chairman knew what a gently spoken, lovely man he was, well that's how I found him and very persuasive. I'm sure he'd done his homework on me. 'Hello David nice to meet you, I was very impressed with your performance, I want to sign you for Cas. and we don't pay backhanders.'

'Well Mr Brunt, in this case we don't have a problem, because if I took a back hander I would owe you something before I've even started work and at my age I don't want to owe you anything.' We chatted more, he was happy I'd agreed no backhander and as long as no money was changing hands then I would sign. It had been arranged already, Trevor Briggs the Castleford winger, for me. I took Doug Alton to one side and insisted that I would only move if my testimonial fund was increased from the £612 to £1,000 he agreed and we shook on it.

I moved to Castleford and Trevor Briggs asked me what I thought of my previous club. 'I think it's going through a transitional time and I can't predict how you will fit in, go and give it a try, if you don't like the set up, don't go.' was the answer I gave. He didn't like the set up and wouldn't sign. Unbeknown to me until some weeks later, Phil Brunt gave Bramley two grand for me. I wrote to Doug Alton requesting that he gave me the money for my testimonial as agreed and was told that he would send it through. It was February 1978.

I do not make these comments lightly but when a player signs a contract, his ambition is only to fulfil it. He is unaware of how the board will fail to honour it if it suits them or their finances at the time. Take for instance the many players who sign contracts with incentive clauses for a certain number of games played in any given season, say 10 for example. If the first player has played nine games and a team-mate on the same contract has only played five and they are both available for selection. On countless occasions the coach will be instructed to choose the second player for the next four games regardless of form or ability. I personally know of many such cases and of coaches who would comply with such requests, sacrificing their integrity on the premise that it's no big deal to them because the players have similar abilities. At three out of the four clubs that I have personally been involved with, I have known this to happen several times. I have also known players actually conspiring to beat this evil practice.

Roy Hawksley, the reserve hooker at Trinity during the 1960's, just happened to be walking past Belle Vue ground as the bus was due to leave for an away game. Geoff Oakes, the first team hooker had a few minutes earlier informed the then coach, Ken Trail, that he was not fit. Ken spotted Roy and shouted him over. 'Get your boots out of the kit room, I can't go into the match without a recognised hooker.' Trinity won and Roy got winning pay plus £500 for 10 games, he gave the winning pay to Geoff. Roy was transferred a while later but for him, justice prevailed and Geoff had shown himself to be a true sport.

Another such occasion was once again at Trinity. Our Malc signed for Trinity in 1957 and completed his apprenticeship with two seasons in the A-team, making his first team debut against Huddersfield in the 1959-60 season. He was an instant success and was a fixture in the team approaching the Wembley final of 1960. Only that was to become a dream to be put on hold because of his wrist and hand injury, the legacy of his car crash that fateful Monday evening, the same evening that our Brian had volunteered to take Malc's two golden Labradors, Old Rex and Young Rex, to the vets to be destroyed for killing hens. The police had made strong recommendations that this action be taken. Wakefield were playing Swinton that night, so Brian took the dogs and Malc went off to play rugby. After the match, he and team mate Albert (Budgie) Firth went out for a drink. Because they had played on the Saturday in the semi-final at Odsal in front of 52,000 fans, drink had been put on hold until after the Monday match. All in all it was a terrible day for our kid, especially as he had been tipped as a certain tourist for that coming summer.

Trinity went on to win the final against Hull at Wembley and five of Trinity's players went on tour that summer and Stuart Hatfield, the Trinity chairman, was tour manager. As a result of the accident, Malc was off work for 10 months and out of the game for 30 months. Wakefield had observed Malc's solicitors request and crossed him off their players register to help with his insurance claim. Malcolm was physically ready to resume his rugby career but was being urged by his solicitor to wait a little longer, the reason being that his claim could double if he held out. Stuart Hatfield wanted him to sign back on straight away and said the club would make up the difference. The family discussed the predicament, Malc was desperate to sign, he had already lost a lot of money in missed wages at work as well as from rugby but in the end he opted to sign back on. He reregistered with Trinity, the insurance company settled and Malc went to see Mr Hatfield, a prearranged appointment. He was in for a shock, Mr Hatfield had found out how much Malcolm had received. 'It's a tidy sum' he pronounced, 'Now let's get you back playing.'

'But you promised me, I settled for less on your promise, the club owes me,' he protested.

'Malcolm, there's an A-team match on Thursday night at Halifax, let's have you back then, OK? You're on our register, we'll not sell you, so put the past behind you.'

When he arrived home Malc was hurt, he told dad, 'I've been double crossed and that's a fact dad.'

'Aye son, tha ought done it wi' a solicitor, but what's done is done. These fellas ah much cleverer than us an' thi don't ev any consciences either, but don't cut off thi nose to spite thi face son, go on Thursday, show um what tha can do an' put it down to experience.'

Malc went on Thursday and played a blinder, he was picked for the first team that same weekend.

Nineteen consecutive games later, he proudly walked out into Wembley's magnificent stadium. We were all there, all the family. You can imagine the ecstasy when Keith Holiday slipped out a magical pass to our kid and he shot in under the sticks, not a hand laid on him, a lead that Trinity built on and a Wembley winner's medal at the end of it. Malc had completed a marathon journey of heartbreaking will-sapping hours of rehabilitation that only he and those close to him could comprehend. He had confounded the specialists who had the audacity to tell a Sampson that he would never wall a brick or play rugby again. Never say never, Malc has left a legacy of houses, bungalows and the odd mansion in his wake, his career spanned nine years with Wakefield then a further six with Bramley. He was due a testimonial the following year after nine years with Trinity but Mr Hatfield told him to move on. He joined me at Bramley in late November 1966, as equally ready to take up the challenge as I had been.

18. That was the Week that was

Through the many years I have been involved with rugby league I saw and experienced an awful lot of things but as a player many demands were made of varying degree's both physical and mental of the athletes of the 1960's and 70's. The one that sticks out like a sore thumb as probably the most callous of acts by the RFL on a club and its players, being deprived of the opportunity to have any chance of reaching Wembley in the Challenge Cup of 1978. Their ruling that Cas travel to Featherstone and fulfil their third round fixture on the Sunday after experiencing a second round tie away at Workington the previous Sunday which Cas drew 8-8. A replay was ordered for Tuesday, hardly two days rest at Cas and that match produced another draw, ironically 8-8 once again. The clubs were ordered to replay Thursday at Wigan, a neutral venue. Cas came good this time scoring twice in the latter stage's of the game winning as I remember 24-14. Three tough 'no quarter asked, none given' cup tie's in five days, only to be ordered to travel to Featherstone come Sunday for the right to progress to the Semi Final. Needless to say the dressing room at Featherstone was like casualty. Mal Reilly had several needles inserted in an egg sized lump protruding from his rib cage, I saw at least five players take the needle others relied on strapping. A good rub down and a wing and prayer hope that fatigue the inevitable enemy would be overcome by desire and carry us through. Alas it was not to be. A narrow defeat and Featherstone progressed. I remember reflecting how unfair it all was, the decision makers pleaded they could do no other, 'The bad weather has created the backlog not us. We can't give special dispensation.'

Cas players to a man did not moan at anytime during that week for it would have been a sign of weakness and loss of dignity but on reflection I have not known of demands before or after, by any team in any sport, being tougher than four cup tie's in eight days. Thank God attitudes have changed in the modern era and such unreasonable challenge's will never happen again.

19. George Bad Benson Says My My Super Ship

Fate is something that may touch someone's life in some way. I believe it was fate that led me into many situations and one in particular springs to mind.

It was a Sunday lunch at the Ship in 1976. Trade had dipped a little since Whitbread's had put me on tanked beer, bitter and mild. I had protested but to no avail they insisted that they knew which way market trends were going and it was the way of the future. Twenty-five years on, how wrong their so-called visionary's have proved to be. However this particular Sunday my jukebox had broken so I brought my music centre down with some ex juke box records and my own collections of LP's. I set it up on a table in the lounge and kept up a constant stream of widely varied music throughout the lunchtime session. The atmosphere was good and so were the beer sales. Several of the soccer lads who were just on their way out at closing commented how much they had enjoyed it and would I be doing the same that night? 'Yes,' I answered sensing it was a leading question, if I was they would come in, if I wasn't they weren't.

Now in 1976, pubs with a disco were uncommon but I duly played music that night and had a few beers. Word spread in the village and by 9 o'clock it was heaving. Fate, luck, call it what you like had opened a door that I wasn't about to close for a long time. The following week I went to Leeds and purchased a set of second hand turntable decks and a few new sounds. Chart singles and new releases I liked or thought might do well. Our Malc's father in law, George was a carpenter, he knocked up a disco console decorating it with coloured Formica off cuts.

Sundays were rolling, parties were being booked for Fridays and Saturdays so it was a natural progression when Wednesdays and Thursdays followed suit.

I then approached our Malc. 'Can we knock this wall out?' I asked. He studied, 'Not a problem I'll measure for the girders and get them delivered Friday morning. You arrange me some labourers ready to start 11.30 Friday night.'

11.30 Friday came, 'Everybody out,' I said. 'We have work to do.' Mel Castle, Johnny Milner, myself, Malc, John Smith, Griss Ansell, we were ready, it had to be seen to be believed. This wall was load bearing internal brick, approximately 10 feet long. 12 o'clock next day girders were in, brickwork and plastering completed. The whole pub was cleaned, dust washed away we were ready for decorating soon as the plaster was dry.

That Saturday people walked in gob smacked. It had opened the pub up enormously and trade shot through the roof. I then decided we needed a major re-furb and extension. Within months, I put in plans to the brewery. 'No cash available,' was the answer. I protested. 'I'm coming out then,' I said. They then came up with fifty percent of the cost. We got the plans passed and went ahead, it was a major effort and we only closed for three days to take out a chimney breast. We now had a major operation, very busy, six nights from seven. We had invested well and we were starting to get a return.

I was loyal to the brewery and purchased everything through them but my rent at this time had risen from £40 per week to £81. Twelve months later the brewery raised it to £141 and despite my protests the following year £180. So much for loyalty. They had invested £10k in 10 years. I was told my sales were among the top 10 of the East Pennines region. Talk about having your nose rubbed in it. When Mavis and I took the pub in 1971, the brewery manager had said it was a good job I played rugby as the income would help my cash flow until we were established and now I felt that they were killing the geese who were laying the golden eggs.

For over 10 years they had enjoyed in excess of 600 barrels per year. Mavis and I were the ones who had ploughed money, time and energy into this property increasing its value threefold but they were still wanting a pound of flesh. I had invested a lot of money into building the business and was becoming more and more disillusioned with the brewery. But life was still good, constantly in the fast lane, coaching the juniors at Stanley, playing rugby, cellar man, DJ, building contractor.

My family were growing up in front of me, us all being together was a bonus. My children were not pub kids. They were rarely allowed to dwell too long downstairs. But they were near to us always and as I say, this is a plus for bringing a family up in this way, also help was at hand for many menial chores, bottling up etc.

By 1984 due to the wear and tear I decided to redecorate and re-furbish. Not too expensive an investment but another kick start. We had our opening night. Big success. Next day we had a visit from the brewery rep. 'I've come to discuss your rent increase David,' he stated.

'But I've got a three year contract and it's only 12 months since you raised it to £240.'

'I'm afraid you're mistaken,' he replied. 'Besides you can afford it and after spending on this recent re-furb your not likely to leave for sometime yet.'

'Oh aren't I?' I replied. 'We'll see about that.'

Two days on they had my notice. Three months later I left the Ship. September 13th 1971 to April 1st 1985. Fourteen of the most wonderful years anyone could wish for. We had packed more living into those years than some people pack in a lifetime, but one thing was for sure, there would be no regrets. No living in the past. We had started another journey. The brewery had been the losers and the pub has struggled to this day to emulate those successful years. Although I have been reliably informed by successive tenants that the brewery carried on using my figures as criteria for setting a rent. This was grossly unfair on the naive unsuspecting incoming tenants. Times were changing. Those days will never be repeated and the pub companies know this.

Those balmy summer evenings from 1971 to 1985 were a bit special but none more special than the Sunday nights when not only had I become a respected DJ (more for the quality of music I played than spiel) but also for the outrageous uniforms I would wear. This lasted for about six months in the summer of 1980. Every Saturday I would visit Homburgs in Leeds the theatrical costume suppliers. The Ship in those days was known over a 15 mile radius as Sammy's Super Ship and we were very busy six nights a week but Sundays were always special. Now in Homburgs, Roger would always have me an outfit ready, always the ship theme and he never repeated one. Horn Blower, Nelson, a Viking and so on. Roger was gay and I know he exacted a lot of pleasure as my dresser but not as much as Mavis my wife who was my undresser, she would occasionally take a photo of me in my full regalia. I would say how do I look and she'd say magnificent, go wow them. Down the stairs I'd go, hovering on the last landing waiting for Ned, Jack, Ken and Harry to look up then I would proceed. They were locals who played dominoes at the bottom of the stairs. Ned was always first to comment, 'Who are you supposed to be this week Sammy?' was the inevitable question. 'Captain Horatio Horn Blower you scurvy dogs,' I replied and I dubbed my hat.

8 o'clock on the dot. I was behind my disco unit always blasting 'My My Supership' a song by George Bad Benson as my opening number, then it was party time right through till 10.30. This particular Sunday I had just finished, the bar was full of empty glasses people were hanging about inside and outside waiting for either a bus or taxi. I was stood at the bar in my resplendent uniform drink in hand talking to the staff when suddenly about six uniformed police came in. One of them I recognised as an Inspector he was tall about 6' 5" he passed me and went to the bar.

'Can I speak to the landlord?' he asked.

'Can I help you Inspector?' I asked.

'Yes you can, this bar is littered with glasses and there's still beer in some, you have people inside milling about, people outside...'

'What the, stop right there!' I quietly but firmly snapped. 'Inspector would you care to follow me?'

Carrying my hat under my arm I proceeded outside onto the beer patio. He followed and we faced each other. I then told him politely, '10 minutes ago I had 250 people in here, it's now 10.45 in another five minutes, two buses one to Rothwell the other to Wakefield and almost everyone will be gone. No fuss, no hassle, no bouncers but if you intend to tear a strip off me I would rather it be out here. I have to empty this place six nights out of seven and if you'd carried on in there my credibility would be shot.

'I'm not sure I like your attitude landlord.'

'Well a captain outranks an inspector, good night Sir,' and I walked back in the pub.

'Cummon get these bloody glasses off bar,' I barked to my bar staff winking at the same time.

Next morning a phone call, I answered. 'Hello! Mr Sampson?

'Yes.'

'Inspector Rose here, would you be good enough to call in at Wood Street Police Station this morning please?'

'Yes certainly,' I replied. 'About an hour OK?'

'Yes fine, just ask for me at the desk.'

'Oh bloody hell I bet I'm for it,' I thought, though I couldn't have been further from the truth. He made me a coffee said he had thought it through and in future co-operation rather than jumping the gun to anonymous calls would be the order of the day. Now that kind of policeman deserves respect he certainly had mine and as I walked down Wood Street I had a spring in my step.

20. Through the Pain Barrier - Physical and Mental

May 1978. Wakefield Trinity at Belle Vue. It was always nice to come back although this was my first time with Cas. I had experienced mixed luck being on the winning side probably three out of ten games with Bramley who over the previous 11 seasons had included many former Trinity men. Our Malc, Keith Holliday, Derek Plumstead, Gerry Mann, Jack Austin, Terry Hopwood and myself and John Woolford was Wakefield born and bred also, so I think it always inspired the others a little to raise their game in support of us, but this time with Cas I felt confident. We had put some good results together and had some real quality players. Steve 'Fizzer' Fenton, John Joyner, Phil Johnson, Terry Richardson, Bruce Burton, Gary Stephens, myself, Bob Spurr, Dave Briggs, Paul Norton, Sammy Lloyd, our coach Mal Reilly and Geoff Wraith another ex Trinity man. Mal had given me my head a little and with these quality players running off me I was playing my best rugby ever and enjoying it to boot.

The game was only about half gone we were just in front about 10-6 when I hit the line turned and off loaded one Wakefield player then I twisted my upper body and John Burke wrapped himself around my legs. Something had to give, it did it was my leg. I was carried off and carted up to hospital. 'Fractured fibula, four weeks in pot,' said the Doc, not as bad as I'd thought, not career threatening, I'd be right for next season.

John Burke came to see me at the pub that night as did the Cas players, bus and all. I was pissed, my pal John Milner filled in as DJ that night. What a party. We won the game too, 38-10 I think. It seems after I'd offloaded, the ball had gone to Fizzer Fenton and he'd scored in the corner. Who says history doesn't repeat itself.

I was ready in time for pre-season training. It was mostly at Kippax and tough. I felt in the best condition I'd been for years, more than holding my own with some much younger lads. The pub was doing well the building business was doing well I was ready for the start of the new season. It was early August and the local village team Stanley Rangers had organized a friendly against the under 18's who were mostly Rodillians rugby union lads. I agreed to play for the Rodillians to help organise them.

The Rangers kicked off to us first play, I called for the ball, the pass was a little slow coming, I was running I caught the ball and as Steve Way came at me my weight was on my right leg as the sole of his boot, size 11, hit my lower shin. They say you could hear the crack up Lee Moor. I hit the floor and knew I wouldn't be getting up, the pain was frightening. I looked at my foot, it was facing the wrong way, at a right angle to my knee. Someone wanted to move me, someone else suggested we wait for the ambulance. I have never been so glad to get to hospital, moving onto the stretcher and the journey was agony. Dad came in the ambulance he always seemed to be there.

When I made my debut at Bramley he was sat in the stand and finished up on the team photo. Ten years on in my testimonial season another team photo, dad's on that one also, he didn't miss many in between either.

As I was wheeled through casualty, I heard the nurse say to dad, 'Wait in there Mr Sampson we'll let you know when you can come through.'

The nurses removed my boot and cut off my sock before the Doc came in, I remember a tall handsome man he started chatting. Turned out he was Australian and loved Rugby. Union was his game, but then I thought you don't get too many doctor's playing league. He explained that after the X-ray's he would have to try and re-position the foot but because I had heavy muscled calves it would be necessary to give me a general anaesthetic. 'Wouldn't have it any other way,' was my reply.

The nurse administered the anaesthetic to a vein in my hand. The Doc ordered everyone, 'You take his other leg. You take a shoulder. You take the other shoulder.' I was surrounded by white uniformed faceless people but something was wrong, I was conscious.

'Doc,' I drawled, 'If you pull on that leg now I don't think anyone will hold me down.' The Doc's face had a look of amazement. He looked across at the anaesthetist she took my hand and injected me again.

Next thing I knew dad was sat at my side as I woke.

'Nah then son I've rung Mavis, they're keeping you in, owt that tha wants son?'

'No thanks dad I'll be ok, I'll be up and about tomorrow, you get yourself off.'

That night I didn't sleep too much but I did get chance to reflect on things, something I rarely had time to do at home.

Next morning, the specialist came to see me. He had treated me before, 'David, you will be going for surgery tomorrow. We are going to plate your leg and it needs a little bit more adjusting.'

'Fine doc,' I replied. 'How long do you reckon?'

'How long do I reckon for what?' He replied.

'Before I'm playing again?' I asked.

He looked at me and paused, looked at the clipboard and looked back at me, 'Your playing days are over David. Besides you're 34, even after recovery you'll be too old to play top level again. Good God man enough is enough.'

'Doctor, I'm 33 (I would be 34 in two days) and are you saying that medically I won't play again or because I'm 33 I'll be too old to come back?'

He took a long look at me. 'Medically it's 50/50 but you're not talking three months or even six months. It will be a long tough road and I don't think...'

I stopped him right there and then. 'Doctor you sort the leg, I'll do the rest and I'm willing to bet you a pint I play first team for Cas again.'

'You're on,' he said.

One hour later the anaesthetist came to see me. 'Hello Mr Sampson. I wonder can you answer me a few questions inreadiness for tomorrow?'

'Sure, take a seat my dear.'

She said, 'To put you out in casualty it took almost 900 milligram's of Pentothal. That's unheard of. Can I ask you, do you like a drink and if so what quantities do you consume per week, bearing in mind that a half pint of beer is one unit how many units would you say your intake was?'

'Oh, about 16 but sometimes more depending on the occasion,' I replied.

'Is that per week?'

'Heck no, that's per day, less if I've been training though.'

'Goodness me. A few more questions and I'll be away and rest assured we'll be ready for you this time.'

The operation went ahead and was successful. They fixed a seven inch plate to my right tibia. Doctor Singh came to see me, he looked at the X-rays. 'It's a bad one David. Bloody crazy if you play again.'

I had many visitors. Mavis was left to run the pub but she came as often as possible. Mal Reilly came too. He assured me my age made no difference. If I got fit that's all that mattered to him. I took encouragement from him. I'll show them I reflected to myself, I'll show them.

The way back was tougher than I ever anticipated. I went through the pain barrier daily. I often felt like giving up but I remembered our Malc and his fight back over two and a half years and I took strength and knuckled down. I got myself back into reasonable condition but I was having back problems. My hip and back were a constant source of discomfort. The specialist told me it was because I was favouring my right leg and causing an imbalance. 'You must do more on your right leg build up, double anything you do on your left.' Eleven months had passed. I was now training well. Pre-season was in full swing. I had to go back to see the specialist. He was impressed. I had a nice tan, the six-pack was visible and I just wanted the all clear.

'Well David, do you still want to play again?'

'Not half doc.'

'Well then we had better get you in and remove that plate then hadn't we?'

This was a bombshell. 'Can't I play with it in?' I asked.

'Absolutely not. We'll take it out. You'll be good as new.'

'How long Doc?'

'Oh, six to eight weeks if all goes well. You've come this far so what's a few more weeks?'

He did the op, gave me the plate as a souvenir and said the bone had healed fine but two months later I was concerned as the wound still hadn't healed. By this time it was about a half inch wide by two inches long and constantly weeping. 'Keep it dry and elevated. The constant swelling of your leg is preventing it from healing.'

The season was now underway. I was very frustrated that an open wound was keeping me out after all I had gone through. I did exactly as I was told and gradually over the next month it healed. I threw myself back into training having fallen behind again. I was desperate to get my pint off the Doc. He along with my brother Malc had been inspirational but I was desperate to get back amongst the camaraderie of the club I had fallen in love with to such an extent that it was my life at that time.

John Sheridan, Mal's assistant coach pulled me over in training. 'You're going well David. When do you think you'll be ready?'

'Who have you got this week?' I asked.

'Hunslet A away' he replied. 'I can sub you and give you last twenty minutes, if you want that is?'

John was one of the nicest and most highly respected coaches in the game and he had constantly encouraged me at the same time as driving his younger players by saying to them quietly, 'He's 35, he should not beat you at anything.' In training his motivational skills were something I admired and learned from.

'OK John, I'll sub. I've never played at Greyhound Stadium.' Hunslet had moved from Parkside my old debut ground.

Well Saturday came and it was a very nervous Dave Sampson when John said, 'You get your tracksuit off Sammy you're going on.' True to his word there were twenty minutes to go.

Playing at prop for Hunslet A that day was a young Stanley lad called Howard Budby. He had initially signed for Leeds from Wakefield. He was a customer in my pub and I later played several seasons alongside him at Stanley Rangers.

I took my first drive as soon as I could. It was my first taste of competitive rugby for 17 months. Howard had deliberately put himself opposite and his tackle came in low. It seemed to take an age for me to hit the floor and I remember thinking, 'Is my leg OK?' Well it was and after that tackle it was all over. I never ever worried again, I thought, 'Now for the first team, a couple more A-team games and I'll be knocking on the door.'

Next morning about 8.30, the phone rang. 'Mal Reilly on the phone,' Mavis shouted. I put my dressing gown on and picked up the phone, 'Hi Mal.'

'Morning mate. How do you feel?'

'Oh I'm fine. I did the last twenty minutes no problems.'

'Yes I know, John's told me. I just wondered if you wanted to come to Wigan with us today?'

'Yes I'd love to. What time does bus go?'

'Half eleven from Cas Bus Station,' came the reply. 'See you there mate.'

I went out for a little jog to get the cobwebs and bit of stiffness out then back for a hot shower and breakfast. I remember thinking what a nice gesture it was of Mal asking me to join them for the day out. Was I in for a shock on arriving at the bus station.

Mal greeted me, 'Thanks for coming David. You sure you're alright?'

'I'm fine mate,' I replied.

'Good then you'll be at number eight. Dave Briggs is injured.' and he walked away with a wry smile on his face.

I was gob smacked, 'I've no boots.'

'They're in basket,' Johnny Ward barked. 'Ger on bus.'

I'd only ever played at Wigan a couple of times before and on arrival I must admit it was awesome. The last time there with Bramley I had scored two tries but we lost 52-10. I looked at their team programme. Steve Breheney was at Number eight. Steve had played for a while with me at Bramley. Mal had told me just concentrate on having a better game than your opposing number. I was comfortable with that. The occasion took away any worries about my leg and we drew 10-10. I played my part, Steve drove the ball in often and I tackled him every time. It was another milestone for me. It was the first time I had drawn winning pay at Wigan and the doctor owed me a pint.

Sure enough I rang him next day and we met at the British Oak. He duly bought me a pint wished me well and went back to the hospital.

The following Friday we played at Cas and won, then the next Tuesday we had the Yorkshire Cup semi against Hull Kingston Rovers. We lost 14-7 it was close though and I remember I should have killed a loose ball, Roger Millward got a foot to it and they went on to score. They also had some very talented young forwards like Len Casey and John Millington. I had suddenly started to feel old.

Next Sunday it was Barrow at home. I had asked Mavis to come along and bring the kids, Dean, Jonathan and Becky. I had made up my mind, the pains were from the inside out very deep and hard to pin point. I was overjoyed with my performance that day. I know I played well but it was time to call it a day at that level. Anyway, Father Time catches up with us all and I felt it was my time.

I explained to Mal and although he would have preferred me to carry on, he respected my decision. When I broke my leg had I not had Mal's encouragement or made the challenge to the doctor then I might not have succeeded. I may easily have become a pot-bellied landlord long before my time and I wouldn't have gone on to play for Stanley Rangers and then coach Cas. The hand of destiny is dealt in strange ways. You take up one challenge, it inevitably opens doors to fresh ones.

The 1981-82 and 1982-83 seasons at Stanley were memorable for me. At last I was giving something back to a game and a village that had given so much pleasure to me. Watching over young players embarking on their careers the intensity was much less demanding at this level but equally rewarding especially when we played at Wakefield in the local cup final at Belle Vue and won 7-6. We took that cup into every pub in the village ending up at the Ship until the early hours.

The following year we lost 6-5 in the same cup final at Belle Vue. Once again, I broke a rib that night which was just before our weekend in London to watch the Rugby Cup Final. I struggled on the journey but the pain subsided as the anaesthetic trickled into my system and I reflected on the many injuries sustained over my career.

Here is the list.

Depressed fractures to both cheekbones

Broken nose (twice)

Broken jaw

Left shoulder (clavicle) fractured

Right shoulder (clavicle) fractured (twice)

Fractured ribs (twice)

Right forearm fractured (four times)

Right fibula fractured

Left tibia and fibula fractured

Bennets fracture to each thumb

First left metacarpal fracture

Second right metacarpal fracture

Left index finger fracture

Displaced vertebrae

Displaced pelvis

Badly torn thigh muscle

Badly torn ankle ligaments

Three front teeth knocked out

21. A Farewell with Dignity

Dad had never been far away from any of us during our sporting careers even as a young 14 year old when I was representing the school at boxing. We had our school championships if you won you were in the school team. I'd won on points against my best mate, Keith Ward, who lived just across the road from me. One fight, one win, school champ at that weight and into the school team.

This particular night in our school gymnasium dad came to watch and I won. After showering I went to sit with dad, the silence was deafening then he quietly asked, 'Do they have ballet dancing at this school ah David?'

'No dad why?'

'Well I think tha would be more suited to it that's all.'

I got the message but his unstinting support since 1956 with first Malc and then both of us had always been that extra inspiration that any athlete would find a bonus. My short journey from Bramley to Cas was a boost to dad. He wasn't so well these days and it wasn't too far to Wheldon Road from Stanley.

Dad had mentioned that he had two uncles who had lived in Cas but he lost touch and years later he had walked to Wheldon Road because someone at work had told him of his uncle living in squalor down there, only to find he had drowned himself in the river a few weeks earlier. He had carried that secret for 40 years and I know it hurt him because it was his father's brother and families and bonding was important to him. He was an only son with two sisters. His father, my grandad Fred, had been a very ill man from the early days of his marriage in 1908 to gran. He died in 1936 aged 56, eight years before I was born and dad never mentioned him unless specifically asked.

After each match with Cas he would quietly sit with his pint and a shandy for me but after I broke my leg dad was never to see me play again. Cancer was diagnosed, even so I still felt that after the operation he would get well, I really did. To me he was invincible.

I went to see him in hospital just after his op and made him show us his scar. Oh he was reluctant, 'Thi mother makes a fuss lads,' I remember him saying but when he opened his pyjama top it came home to me. They had cut him in half, more than half. He saw the shock on my face. 'How's the leg ah David?'

'Oh I'm mending dad. Won't be long.'

He was later discharged and seemed to be on the mend, going out for a drink, having a bet and in good spirits. I remember thinking, 'I knew he was invincible.' Then on November 28th mum rang, 'Can you call down before you go training about 5 o'clock?'

'Yes mum course I can.'

When I got there our Malc was already in the lounge, sat in the shotgun chair, mum and dad were on the settee. I sat on a buffet next to Malc. Just us two, Brian was over in Bingley and mum told the girls individually except Maire. She was in Canada now. Mum was between dad and us and she proceeded, 'Your dad wants you to know that the specialist has given him three weeks at most and he would like to spend as much time as possible with you. He'll answer any family questions you might ask so as it's passed down to his grand-children and he doesn't want you worrying or making a fuss.' dad had never spoke a word as always even with such a momentous statement it was through mum.

'What can we do dad, what can we do?'

Dad uttered his first words, 'Well its Wetherby Races tomorrow. I'll not better risk waiting til Boxing Day's meeting, a would like mi three sons an can we make room for Jack Shaw. I'd like to take Jack.'

'Consider it done.'

'Well ah David get thi sen off training. I'll see you both tomorrow.'

John Sheridan noticed I wasn't performing well in training.

'Having problems wi leg Dave?' He asked.

'No John, leg's fine.' I proceeded to get things off my chest. I was struggling to accept the reality of it all and felt I should be with Dad.

'I'm sure that even now thi dad knows best Dave that's why he wants you to train, not sit moping. Dig deep and do your best.' I did.

Next day we duly met and had a wonderful day out. A couple of win-ners each so it wasn't too expensive but it was dad's dry humour that constantly kept our spirits up. One particular horse ran badly, 'I'll never back that bloody thing again.' or when the raffle girls were selling tickets in the pub, 'Do you want to have a go?' They said to dad.

'When's it drawn?' dad inquisitively asked.

'About one hour,' came the reply.

'Oh well I'll have a quids worth then.' All tongue in cheek and not too often to appear patronising.

When I dropped him off at 1 Moorhouse Avenue he turned and said to me, 'Nah then ah David I understand you've been given the task of ringing our Maire in Canada?'

'Yes dad.'

'Well I just want you to tell her that when I was a young man playing dominoes I would brag if I get three score years and ten you'll not hear mi complain. But I never thought he would take me at mi word.' Dad was 70.

That was a very difficult phone call I had to make. Maire flew home immediately.

Griss Ansell called into see dad. 'Leah,' dad went on to say, 'Get me that carrier bag aht coal house will you?'

Mum came back. 'This one?' she said.

'Yes, what size boot are you Griss?'

'Nine and a half George.'

'Just as a thought. They're brand new I'm not going to need em and I can't think of a better man who'll do them justice.' Griss was a labourer with our Malc and he wore those boots until they fell off. Dad had loads of callers but they only came the once and all parted with practically the same words, 'See you George.' 'Thanks for calling Eric, Jack,' whoever. It was always the same, I believed then and still do that even in those final days dad was teaching us his last lesson, a lesson in dignity. He asked mum that when he went, to pin his rosette 'I didn't vote for Maggie' on his chest and nail the lid down. On January 14th, 1980 mum did. I was 36 he was just 71.

When he had gone I realised that there was so much to say, I now sing the song living years by Mike and the Mechanics better than anyone else in the world and that's a fact. Well I think so and I know he hears me because the words are so prophetic.

Every generation blames the one before

And all of their frustrations come beating on your door

I know that I'm a prisoner to all my father held so dear

I know I'm a hostage to all his hopes and fears

Just wish I could have told him in the living years

22. The Serpent of Albi

It was a lovely spring day in 1983. I was stood enjoying the panoramic view from the top of a hill in Castelnau. Mrs Bonifous had taken myself, Dean my son and her son Christophe out for the afternoon. She had told me it was one of her favourite beauty spots and I had to agree. It was truly magnificent, one of many in that part of France.

We were enjoying the hospitality of these wonderful people by way of an exchange trip from Stanley Rangers Juniors to Albi, a beautiful historic town in the Languedoc Region near Toulouse. These exchange trips had been reciprocal annually for several years, in fact it was my second visit.

The two lads decided they would climb the tower, an ancient stone monument with an internal spiral staircase leading to the top. It was approximately 70 feet high and had been used in the Middle Ages as a lookout post across the lush perfectly flat plateau. I took one look inside and elected to stay out. It was a tight squeeze. The dear boys waved from a small oblong window and then carried on to the top.

Christophe was a tall handsome boy with a flock of black hair. He played loose forward. Our Dean was staying with his family I was in a hotel. Mrs Bonifous had invited us for tea later.

That afternoon, the boys were waving and shouting for a few moments only before making their way back down. Christophe emerged first and with his Mum made his way to the car. I waited at the entrance for Dean. Out he came and the first thing he said was, 'Look dad,' and he proffered his arm palm upturned towards me. I took a closer look, there were two tiny puncture marks on the front of his wrist about a centimetre apart. I made the comment that he had probably been stung or bitten by an insect. He rubbed it and we made our way to the car.

It was about 1.30 and Mrs Bonifous said she wanted to call at the supermarket. The boys took turns riding on the trolley then we loaded the car then set off back for the rest of the journey home. Dean mentioned that he felt sick, we all laughed and accused them of drinking too much wine after the previous evening's match. The boys protested that they had only had a couple of glasses. Dean said, 'I'm going to be sick.' I pulled two French loaves out of the carrier and handed him the bag and he proceeded to be violently sick, so much so that I was alarmed. He half filled the bag. I said, 'How do you feel now?' 'Oh a lot better for that.' Mrs Bonifous laughed and blamed the booze. She didn't believe them about the two glasses, nor did I.

We arrived back at the house which was a delightful detached property. Mr Bonifous was carrying two pheasants across the back garden. He waved and Mrs Bonifous tried to explain that he was going to kill them for our tea. I went into the garden for closer inspection. He hand reared everything, rabbits, pheasants, turkeys, pigeons. There was at least a dozen of each.

My French was limited so communication was difficult but Christophe acted as interpreter best he could. Dean said he did not want any food as the aroma drifted from the kitchen. Dean then went outside and sat on the wall. I followed. 'What is it Son, what's the matter?'

'I feel terrible and we really did only have two wines last night.'

'Let me look at that arm again.' There was slight swelling and reddening around the two punctures. I called Mrs Bonifous. We had said nothing to her previously but I voiced my concerns because Dean was now sweating and had gone a pale grey in colour. Mrs Bonifous said, 'Get in the car, we'll go to the doctors.' This was another 20 minute car journey. Dean was drifting so I kept talking to him and told him to fight it. 'Don't you go unconscious on me.'

Soon as we arrived at the docs he laid Dean out. I tried to explain about the marks but the doc didn't seem to think they were relevant. Now the doc didn't speak much English neither did Mrs Bonifous and we had left Christophe back at the house in our haste. The doc started pressing Dean's abdomen, 'I sink possibly appendix problem. Appendix Monsieur Sampson.'

I wasn't having any of that I thought. 'No no problem appendix I took hold of Dean's arm. 'Problem here,' and I pointed to his wrist. 'Problem here,' I protested.

The doc quickly spoke in French to Mrs Bonifous but I picked up enough to know he was sending for an ambulance. 'OK OK I understand.'

The ambulance wasn't too long, about 20 minutes so I reasoned that it would take another 20 to reach hospital, that would make it 5 o'clock, three and a half hours since we had left Castelnau. Dean was in and out of consciousness as he was put in the ambulance. I was not allowed in so I followed with Mrs Bonifous. She was fearless and kept right up the backside of the ambulance all the way into Albi and to the hospital. It was the worst 20 minutes of my life worrying how I could communicate in the hospital. During the car journey I had asked if there were any snakes in this part of the world and she laughed out, 'Serpent dormeur.' It took ten minutes of our journey to establish that the snakes were all in hibernation. She assured me, 'No possible, no possible.'

Reaching the hospital and seeing Dean wheeled away it occurred to me that I must have an interpreter or I might not see him alive again. My worst fears came true when after 20 minutes a Doctor came to me and asked if Dean my son had any history of appendicitis, now he said it in French but I understood him. 'No,' I said, 'Appendicitis impossiblay,' which I know was Spanish but my frustration was beginning to show. I pointed to my wrist, 'My son mon fer ere le serpent possibly.' Just then another doctor walked in, he looked and listened then came across, 'Your French is very good Spanish Sir, can I be of assistance?' I quickly explained, he in turn spoke in French of my insistence. He then stated he would deal with the case himself, not to worry and he would be back shortly. I paced around the casualty department.

He returned and spoke, 'We are treating your son for the bite of a snake. You were correct but I can understand my colleague's reluctance to accept it because there are only two puncture marks when normally there are three also these two are close together. Your son has explained that on his way down the tower he had his palm to the wall so the bite was not complete. The bottom fang must have missed locking in, the width of the top fangs indicate it was only a youngster, probably in a nest in a hole in the wall.'

He went on to explain, 'It is lucky you got him here in time. It is also very lucky it was not the mother. They will have been in hibernation all winter and the stored venom would be very toxic. The fact that it took five hours to recognise and treat could have been too late, as it is he will make a full recovery in a few days.'

Dean did fully recover but I never saw any pheasant dinner. Apparently when Mrs Bonifous arrived home late that evening Christophe and Mr Bonifous had scoffed the lot.

When Mal Reilly walked into the Ship with two young ladies it would certainly have raised a few eyebrows but this time he was chaperoning. It was mid week and the girls were staying with Mal and Sue. 'Take us somewhere lively,' they had asked him. Fate I later reflected.

The girls were on the dance floor and Mal and myself were chatting. Since I'd retired at Cas we had met occasionally socially. It was during this conversation I had stated my intention to retire from amateur rugby. 'I'm almost 40. I'm still fit enough but I've got all my coaching badges so I think I'll apply for an A-team job somewhere. If I don't I will finish up turning out another season with Stanley and I don't want that.'

Mal replied, 'Do me a favour David just hold tight for a couple of weeks will you?'

He didn't elaborate and I knew not to ask.

Two weeks later I received a phone call from the then chairman Gordon Appleyard. 'Geoff Wraith has resigned as A-team coach David and Mal's asked me to ring. Are you interested?'

I did not hesitate, 'Of course I am Gordon.'

'Dun't pay much tha knows,' he bluntly barked.

'Gordon if I'd been in game for money I would have packed in years ago.'

'OK, I'll call and see you again soon.'

At my first training session the players assembled on the training pitch, I knew most as I'd only been away three years. Mal proceeded to lead the players on a lap of the perimeter. I stood with John Walker.

Approaching me for another lap Mal called, 'Hey David aren't you going to join us?' I did and every session thereafter.

I trained just as a player all that pre-season and I vividly remember Kev Beardmore's words on completing a team relay when I held off Dave Finch to win for our team. 'We might not be best team in rugby but we have fittest coaching staff.'

I knew then I had earned the players respect especially the younger ones whom I would be coaching. I particularly recall that these were good times both rugby wise and socially. Myself, Mal and John Joyner had developed an affinity and belief that even during these early days of coaching we were capable of achieving something big.

For myself with the second team, I coached some talented committed youngsters and a few veterans such as Barry Higgins, Steve Gill and John Kear. In that time we twice won the Yorkshire cup and finished our Wembley season as joint league leaders only beaten for the title on points difference.

As with most coaching jobs at that time we were poorly rewarded financially but the cameraderie and memories were priceless.

23. Wembley 86

Many players throughout their careers dream of Wembley. The magic of the Challenge Cup. The honour of walking in single file out of the famous tunnel to the tumultuous applause of the fans. The most spectacular event in the long history of our domestic competition.

Our Malc had achieved this in the 1963 final against Wigan and I always wanted to emulate him. Every year I believed that a miracle was possible but as a player like many others, I was destined to be a nearly man. 1964-65 Hunslet beat us in the semi, 1969-70 Cas had signed Tony Thomas after failing to land me then proceeded to notch up two visits. Then 1978 when Featherstone beat us in that epic fourth game Sunday to Sunday quarter final week.

I had been a pro 18 years and almost all of it first grade, but it was not to be. Year after year I had to settle for the annual trip with the lads, sometimes by bus, sometimes by train, sometimes making it back the same day, sometimes not. Then when the day trips stopped we'd go for the weekend. It would be one long party but when those players walked onto that pitch, I knew for them too it was a dream coming true and I always remember thinking, 'Savour it, enjoy it lads, I would.'

At one time I think I was a little jealous of some players, feeling maybe they'd had more than their share of luck. One player made his debut at Wembley and never played for the first team again another playing only his seventh game, but as I grew older I learnt to accept that being in the right place at the right time was not to be envied. We were all in the same game.

My time in its own way did arrive and I was lucky enough to have the experience to enjoy it. It was the 1985-86 season's Challenge Cup final against Hull Kingston Rovers. I was now with John Kear, assistant to Mal and we made a good coaching team.

Mal wanted no stone unturned for that final and his preparation was meticulous. We were the underdogs and that's how Mal wanted to play it. However, Mal always believed that we would win, in fact he even wrote his victory speech the night before at the dressing table in our room. When he delivered it at the winners reception no one expected the thoroughness and hard thought that he'd put into his speech, it was indicative of the man at work.

Mal always led by example and he delivered a team of winners. The closeness of the Challenge Cup result did not matter to any of us, although one director rocked the boat saying after the speech, 'If Dorahy had kicked that goal it would all have been so different.' He knew that had touched Mal.

'Take no notice Mal,' I whispered, 'I think he's jealous of you, this is your night relax and enjoy it.'

Sure if Dorahy's goal had gone over we would have lost by one point but my philosophy was because our defence had worked so hard the corner was the only place we allowed them to score and it made the kick that much more difficult. Our players were still giving a hundred percent at the death for themselves, for Mal, for the fans and for the directors, yes the very same man who had tried to sour Mal's moments of glory. Thankfully, Mal treat the statement with the contempt it deserved. He too was still learning.

Every final has its own identity. One would expect a close encounter every time with such a coveted prize at stake and this final lived up to the occasion. The traditional intense rivalry of both teams brimming with match winners and comparable overseas talent in their ranks. If there was to be a deciding factor known to anyone before the kick off then they must have had a crystal ball.

Gary Lord had got the nod over Dave Rookley at full back. Hull KR put up several early bombs to test Gary, probing, searching for a weakness. Rovers' Gavin Miller shadowing Ian French and likewise to the extent of cancelling each other out. Only something of extraordinary skill or vision would ever have separated the two teams that day. Cas fans might argue it was John Joyner finding the space to release Jamie Sandy for an incredible try others would credit the mighty Kevin Ward in releasing Tony Marchant for another, or the try and goals from Bob Beardmore. In conclusion it took special talent to create and to finish and defend.

History tells us that if John Dorahy had kicked that goal in the dying seconds it would have been amongst the greatest kicks of all time but he failed and truth is that was the clinical cruel difference between Cas and Hull KR in that 1986 Wembley epic. That does not detract from anyone's contribution throughout that long journey especially that of Mal Reilly's and when I read of the panel who interviewed him recently for the post he truly deserved, the GB Supremo. I shook my head in disbelief. It should have been him interviewing them as to their suitability to work alongside him to lead our country against the archenemy. I truly believe that power brokers from high, the Super League paymasters from the antipodes have far too much say in the future of our game.

I don't think that I am a sad former player or bitter coach as is often aimed by the young of today. But I believe no successful general of the great campaigns of the past ever spread his forces as thinly as have our recent leaders in Super League. I do feel the game of today has its merits but there are cracks appearing. The drying up of Murdoch's money will have disastrous effects as players and their salaries are collectively reduced in the manner that the Northern Ford Premiership did a couple of seasons ago. Even after this action the NFP are still on shaky ground with many clubs in serious financial difficulties or losing their momentum by bad planning. Personally I watch the Aussie rugby on Sky and this is the worst season of viewing I have ever endured. Its entertainment value is minimal and falls far short of our domestic competition and yet we still see fit to ignore building up our future around one of our own.

I do not want to appear all doom and gloom in fact the British Amateur Rugby League Association appears stronger than ever, Junior Rugby is booming and the Conference is a superb concept. In fact I advocate we should establish a fast track development programme where professional players who have learnt their trade are able to take up posts as player coaches on subsidised salaries at Conference clubs. The funding for this would come from the joint coffers of Super League and the Rugby Football League.

This together with national coverage and sponsorship should be vigorously pursued as should our overseas programme.

I have read recently that all our overseas development could flounder because of the financial disaster of the World Cup. Lets stop bleating and berating one another and find these countries interim payments to keep them afloat. Or have we already spread our finances so thin that it is too late? If that's the case then bring someone to book.

24. I'm Going to be a Pro

'David!' I remember Mavis shouting, 'Will you come up?'

'Oh what will it be now?' I thought as I went upstairs.

We lived in the Travellers at this time and on reaching the top Mavis added, 'I'll go look after the bar, I want you to have a word with your son.'

'My son eh? That means prepare yourself.' I walked into the lounge. Dean was stood by the window. 'OK son what am I to have a word with you about?'

He hesitated then blurted, 'I've given notice at work, I'm packing in.'

I closed the door behind me, 'Sit down,' I asked. I sat in my chair opposite. 'Right fill me in. What's brought this on?'

Dean soon relaxed. I'd thought he was expecting a confrontation instead I realised that this just might be a momentous decision and a rational debate was needed. He poured out the facts, 'It's like a prison. I feel I'm doing a sentence. I know I'm learning a trade but I won't spend my life doing it so it seems so pointless.'

Dean worked at Yorkshire Imperial Metals in Leeds as a trainee fitter. In another 18 months he would have served his time, done his apprenticeship that is. He like me would have a trade. I reflected to myself, 'It's what I wanted from him. It's what his grandad would have wanted but I quickly checked my train of thought. He's gone 18 years old. He is intelligent and articulate. It must be what Dean wants.' So with these thoughts it prompted a furtherance of the conversation. 'Alright son, tell me something what are you going to do with your working life?'

'I'm going to be a professional rugby league player,' came the answer. No frills just those nine words.

I couldn't help feeling a gush of respect and admiration come over me and I instinctively took the bull by the horns. 'Right OK son,' I asserted, 'I'll run with you on this one. You say you've given one months notice so for the next fortnight I'll set you a training schedule. If you adhere to it without fail, I'll give you my blessing. If you don't, you complete your apprenticeship, agreed?'

'Agreed.'

I then proceeded to explain what it would take. He hadn't even had an offer to sign professional but this would be his make or break year. 'Dean the pluses are your enthusiasm, physical stature and you're a Sampson but those three things alone will not take you where you want to go. It will be foolish to chase shadows at this stage of your career, in comparison to myself, Uncle Malc and even Uncle Brian. Your skill level, speed of thought, vision and pace leaves you with a mountain to climb. I hope I never have to lay this on you again but talking a big game has to be backed up with the stamina and commitment to play one.'

I recollected when I had been turned down at Wakefield and the subsequent training programme our kid had put me through and I poured it out to him. 'To achieve your goal you must be the fittest. The skills will develop in time, the vision comes with experience but to ever tread the path long enough to develop those skills your strength, power and stamina must dramatically improve. As of tomorrow you'll cycle to work in the morning and run home at night. You must use the clock, log your times and you must never ever do a slower time than the day before. The day after you'll run to work and cycle home. Keep a diary and if you cheat with the pen you will ultimately fail with your goal.'

Well it was seven miles from the Trav's to work, my Son did every session and we built on that stamina base. His mum wasn't too pleased at first but she came around. Yorkshire Imperial Metals loss was Dean Sampson's gain and 12 months later he accepted an offer from Castleford.

His grandad I know would have been so proud of us both. For me showing tolerance and understanding and to Dean for showing commitment to the task set. He was to make mistakes in the future like his father and grandfathers but I was determined that he would receive support understanding and forgiveness. That is his right.

Dean's determination and enthusiasm were the first attributes that were noticeable on the rugby field. As a junior player he would have played three games a day. He would follow the older boy's teams always with a kit bag ready just in case they were short. I remember one particular Saturday morning game at Wyther Park Leeds v Stanley under 14's, Dean was 10. We were short by one player no subs. I let him play and he got a blooded nose but made his Dad proud. I also remember him one Sunday morning at Garforth. He was 14, I was playing with our Sunday open age team and once again we were one short so I picked him on the wing. I had played the day before for the Saturday side but the aches and pains were soon forgotten in realising my obligations to him. As it happened the game was tight. We were a few points down with a few minutes to go. I spied a weak spot and Dean read my play.

The report in the Express the following week read '...*Dave Sampson switched the play and passed to D Sampson who dived over in the corner for a try. Dave Sampson converted to win the game...*'

Two years later at 16, Dean played Saturday league open age at Sharlston, something I never achieved. Johnny Wolford guested for Stanley that day. The report fed back to me was your Dean played a blinder. I made further enquiries. It was Johnny's supreme ball skills that had put Dean through the gaps like only Johnny could.

Dean went down to Cas the following season. It was a natural progressive move. I was coaching the Seconds and Dennis Hartley was coaching the Colts. I knew Dennis would improve Dean's game immensely although he had already achieved more than I could have hoped for playing for Yorkshire and England Junior Schools.

I remember insisting to him, 'Listen to your coach and learn, you have one of the finest props ever to play this game as your guv'nor. He can teach you so much.' and he did.

Dean blossomed gradually with the Juniors and Colts and attracted the attention of several other clubs but to Dean there could be no other club. He like I loved everything about Cas and he signed in 1986 for a grand. 'That's all I'll pay,' David Poulter had stated. Well it was double what Gary Hetherington with Sheffield had offered so it was really no contest although I remember Dean being flattered by Gary's attention.

Dean went on to join me with the A-team and this was a very rewarding year. This time the boot was on the other foot when we turned out together because we were short against Keighley at Cas in the cup which in itself was a memorable achievement. I was the sub this time and he was looking out for his dad.

Few fathers have been fortunate enough to play at a professional level with their sons. Dennis Hartley springs to mind as one and Jeff Grayshon with his son at first grade level, another. Such lucky dad's can appreciate the satisfaction it brings, albeit short lived it was special. It was equally rewarding when Dean went on to get a team player of the season and man of the match against Hunslet in the Yorkshire Cup Final at my old club Bramley's Mclaran Field.

That summer Mal Reilly was to accept the Great Britain post and I was to accept the first team job. I remember Mal saying, 'I'll have to find a new mate now.' Those years we had been together were special to me. We went our separate paths leaving only memories to savour and I often do.

Coaching and being a coach involves many difficult decisions. In the many years I coached, probably my most difficult and somewhat controversial decision was choosing my own son to make his debut for the first team. Castleford v St Helens, the opening match of my first season in charge.

I had been Mal Reilly's assistant for three years. He had gone and I was attempting to replace him, a man of whom I had the greatest respect and admiration. I had learnt so much from him and although I was four years older, his maturity had seen him through many testing situations. Mal would often ask me for my opinion then make his decision. Many times we were parallel in our appraisals of say picking a team. One thing that springs to mind was the Wembley Team of 1986, his 15 was two different to me. He chose and we won 15-14.

I had my assistants and I would use them. John Kear and Mick Morgan were both knowledgeable and I had the utmost respect for them. I argued against starting Dean but neither agreed. 'He's been outstanding in two pre-season friendlies and in his training. He's earned it David,' they argued. I made the point for two other players both of whom subsequently asked for a move on not being selected. In the end I went with Dean and just to add pressure to the situation the press made a meal of the double debut.

One player stormed out got in his car and sped out of the stadium. Another came to see me and asked for a transfer. 'Welcome to the hot seat' I thought.

Well Dean started, it was a tough close game and he was holding his own. I remember the game was about 60 minutes old and the score 8-8. Cas were attacking 25 metres from the St Helens line, 20 metres from the main stand playing towards the Wheldon Road end. Kev Beardmore went to dummy half. Dean came on the burst. He thought Kev was about to use him as a dummy runner and miss him out but Kev's ability to make lighting quick decisions came to the fore. He gave Dean the ball just before the gain line. Dean hit the first line at full pace. He burst through the tackles of Andy Platt and Chris Arkwright then side stepped off his right foot, brushed aside an attempt by Phil Veivers at full back and put the ball under the sticks one handed, reminiscent of his Uncle Malc at Wembley in 1963 against Wigan.

I was sat in the main stand. Mal Reilly was one row in front. We had jumped up simultaneously along with the whole stand. He shook my hand and said, 'I'm so pleased for you mate.' We went on to win the game and I reflected to the victor goes the spoils.

At the time of penning this account, Dean requires about two games to achieve 400 appearances for Castleford. A milestone for any player but especially a prop. So between the three of us John Kear, Mick Morgan and myself I think we can feel happy about that decision back then knowing we got it right.

My mandate for my first season in charge from David Poulter was to bring on the youngsters who I had coached to success in the second team and establish them as first team players. 'Stay up in the top division and anything else will be a bonus.'

This was a transitional time, let's remember Mal had been at the club 13 years and a lot of people were set in their habits. I knew it would take longer than one season to move forward with the times. Something Mal or any other coach would have had to face. I set about the task full of enthusiasm. We reached the Yorkshire Cup Final against Bradford at Elland Road. We drew 12-12. I felt we should have won. There was a brawl just before half time and I feel this upset us more than them.

In the replay we suffered a couple of injuries to influential players and lost a close game at Headingley. Both games were well supported and maybe with hindsight I thought my bonus was already in the bag. We achieved a record score against Swinton, beat both Hull sides home and away and won through at home against Wigan without any overseas players.

We had nine young players that featured in 15 games or more and on a trip to France we beat Halifax in Albi. In the British Coal Nines, we were only beaten by Wigan in the final away at Central Park.

We had an unfortunate away defeat at Wigan in the Challenge Cup, a game we almost and should have won. This was probably my biggest single coaching disappointment. We had worked all week on my theory that Wigan's strong defence would not be able to cope at defending against their own moves and I was proved right. We scored four tries all of them copycat moves and had it not been for Bob Lindner spending 10 minutes in the sin bin and a magnificent Henderson Gill tackle on Johnny Fifita, our season could well have kick started again. As it was it did not. We squeezed into seventh and got stuffed at St Helens in the playoffs.

It was in the dressing room that David Poulter told me the club would not be renewing my contract. I wasn't in the mood for protesting that I had more than achieved my goals set at the start of the season or that I had also sold several players to balance the books financially. I accepted it. I quietly got on the bus and went straight home.

What had hurt most was the fact that David had asked me not to attend the supporters function at the Civic Centre the next night. I did not get a chance to air my views or answer questions. It was if they wanted to bury me. I went into myself for the next three days or so.

I had insisted that Dean and Mavis go to the function. I felt it would help Dean long term. He had wanted to pack in when he arrived home. 'I'll not accept that sort of talk. I will rise to the challenge and so must you. We will help each other and survive.' I remembered what my Dad had once quoted to me and I passed it on once more. 'Dean, it's about being and becoming and this is what's in front of us both.'

The phone calls I received over the next few days were of great encouragement to me. Peter Smethurst from Swinton, a man I had never spoken to in my life, a stalwart player in his era, and he cared enough to ring as did Mal Reilly and many more. Their encouragement enabled me to shake off the depression and Wednesday I was out training with a new found determination and will to survive.

25. I Could Play Until 40

People will sometimes make the comment that Dean has not been given fair recognition when it comes to Great Britain caps. I would concur but I also acknowledge his development years were severely curtailed by the presence of Lee Crooks at Cas and Darryl Van de Velde's opinion that Dean must just cart the ball up as a number 10. Lee Crooks was a skilful ball player in the forwards and this is no criticism of Darryl who always called it as he saw it. A team must have a blend and Dean was encouraged by myself that Darryl was his boss and he must satisfy him. He must have done this to a certain extent because he was rarely out of the squad.

However, when Stuart Raper came along, Dean was allowed to express himself and I will never forget attending the Past Players Association Dinner of 1997 when the chairman Alan Hardisty announced the Player of the Year award. He stated, 'In our opinion this award goes to a man who clearly was the difference between Castleford staying in Super League or relegation. That man gentlemen was Dean Sampson.'

Dean was not at the dinner for some reason which escapes me but I was asked to collect the award on his behalf. It was the proudest moment of my sporting life.

His Grandad would have been proud, his father was and so was he when I gave him the trophy. Dean was now 30 and I know the adage that props develop late but I could not see the hierarchy rebuilding a new Great Britain team on the back of 30 year old prop. One pleasing aspect is he has maintained his form, fitness and enthusiasm. It will therefore be a dammed shame if people write Dean's career off because of his age rather than his performances.

Kevin Ward's career was curtailed at 37 but it took a horrific broken leg to bring his retirement about. His body and mind wanted more. Jeff Grayshon played some of his best rugby in his mid to late thirties and Karl Harrison was 36 before deciding on a coaching career.

Let's hope Dean takes a leaf from their book. Mal Reilly gave me the carrot all those years ago when I joined Cas from Bramley. I hope someone offers Dean one but if it's not to be, he's a talented coach already. So maybe this is where his future lies. I will remind him of the seeds of hope and the new rose each year.

26. Life after Cas

After Castleford I went to the doctors. He diagnosed high liver blood count, no booze for three months, 'That's why you have been feeling tired and listless.' Even so three months off the drink was a tall order for a landlord. I took up the challenge, I had promised Dean. I trained every day for three months, sometimes twice a day, gym, cycling, running, swimming, I felt younger than my 44 years. Mum wasn't well this summer, cancer had been diagnosed and she'd refused an operation. Mum reasoned it didn't do dad much good. I was also using this as a driving force. The doc had said, 'Another three months, you are not clear yet.' so I continued.

August came I had to attend a coaching course in Loughborough. I'd booked on a refresher course for one week. Mum had told our Connie how proud she was of me not drinking but she was going downhill fast. I was concerned that we might lose her while I was away for the week. Now she'd been giving me the words of a song for several weeks that dad used to sing to her when they were courting, I'd promised to learn it and sing it for her and it would forever be my song. The song was Sunshine of Your Smile. Once when Daley Thompson was in the bar he'd quoted it was also his mum's favourite.

We had a good week. I roomed with John Kear and Kevin Tamati was in the next room. We had some good laughs, Kevin's songs were easy listening too. Kevin, a proud Maori and legendary player, had a fine voice.

I had rung home everyday and mum was fading and at the end of the week I drove home and went to see her, she looked weak and so tiny. Connie closed the door leaving us alone together whilst I sat holding her hand and she looked up at me, 'Ah David,' she said, 'Nice to see you.'

'And you mum.'

'Av you learnt me song?' She whispered in a frail voice.

'I have mum, all of it. I'll try sing it to you softly.'

'Dear face that holds so sweet a smile for me
Were you not mine how dark this world would be
I know no light above that could replace
Love's radiant sunshine in your dear dear face.'

I sang the chorus softly and then the second verse. She smiled. 'That was lovely' whispered mum in an every weaker voice. 'I'm so proud of you.' She closed her eyes and squeezed my hand. Next day I could not visit but Tuesday when I called, Connie told me, 'Mum's gone David, go up love.' Mum looked at peace.

When I came downstairs, Connie said, 'After you left Sunday David she never woke up, it was if she had given up and happily gone to sleep. She passed away some twenty minutes ago.' I was sad but glad I'd made her happy. She deserved so much more for she had always given more than she had taken from life.

As for me I had lost my mum and the Cas job all in six months but I was fit and I had decided to play one season only with Stanley Rangers. I needed to regain my self-respect. I earned my place and played 28 games. It was like I had been reborn at the age of 44. Each week I would turn up with my bag, boots and all, enjoying each match as if it were my last. Travelling to some new teams and clubs long established in the amateur game. If I met faces from the past to enjoy a drink with after the game I would deem it a bonus. The down side would be the occasional young upstart wanting to make a name for himself.

We were playing Sharlston at home. Long-term fierce rivals another village steeped in the tradition of miners and rugby league and this particular player was propping opposite myself. The first scrum down we locked in when suddenly I spotted a right hook coming my way. I lifted my chin instinctively and WHACK! Rusty Gardner my hooker was the painful recipient. I broke from the pack and drew back my right arm fist clenched about to deliver retribution. All this in the blink of an eye but my punch was to land after Rusty's left hook, which opened the opposing prop's eye like slicing a melon. Little did he know Rusty Gardner was an ex-army boxing champ and he too the son of a miner.

The Sharlston prop spent some time on the touchline and when returning to the fray I was impressed with his new found respectful approach to scrimmaging. Dad had always maintained the bully will always back down to meaningful confrontation. I always found this to be true whether in the pub or on the sporting arena. One of the rewarding things after such encounters was the hospitality shown and expected in the pub after these local derbies. Afterwards it was back to the Travs. Mavis and myself were 'mine hosts' and the ale would flow until closing and sometime's after.

I was no longer in the professional game and come Christmas, the Travs was very busy. Boxing Day gave me the opportunity to go watch our Dean playing at Cas. 11 o'clock kick off. After the match I had a couple of drinks and drove back to the pub. I was working as Boxing Day was always busy and we would only close around 5.30 to clean up. This we did but I was asked by Curly Gibb, 'David, any chance you can drop me off in Cas to pick up my car? Our kid left it this morning and I need it.' Curly was a smashing lad the son of my good friend Alan Gibb. A man who will be well remembered for serving BARLA for many years. Well I'd only had a couple of halves because we had been so busy I was planning a good drink that night. Cas wasn't far, Just one junction down the motorway and Curly's car was sat all alone in a car park.

I set off back home and as I pulled onto the motorway I thought, 'I'll get back quick as I can to help Mavis and the kids clean up.' I eased my foot onto the accelerator 60-70-80, I was cruising at 80 for the short distance to junction 30. I eased off at the slip road and turned left for Wakefield when would you believe it. Yes, you've guessed, alongside me was a motorway police car. From nowhere he had suddenly appeared. 'Pull over into the lay-by,' he signalled. As it happens this lay-by was just about where I'd seen that rabbit about 25 years previously. I reflected that was a bad day and I think this will be.

Now I'm sure everyone knows how it works. There were two of

them, one is as nice as pie the other is the bully. Well I wasn't in the mood for a bully as he found out. My reasoning was apart from being disappointed I knew my previous convictions had lapsed. I had a clean licence and I could do 12 months ban no problem, so I decided that first time I'd done the urine sample the second time the blood sample so this time I would refuse both. That way I would have a round robin up.

I wasn't flippant nor did I want to appear disrespectful but December has never been my favourite month. My dad used to make me cry singing 'He's the little boy that Santa Claus forgot.' Then when I was 19 he did forget. Not one present that particular Christmas plus I'd been pulled for my third breathalyser, all in bloody December. I made a promise to myself I'll never get pulled again in December and I never did.

I pleaded guilty and duly did my 12 months ban. For some unknown reason I had to attend Wetherby Court House. Soon as my case came up one of the magistrates stood down, 'I've known Mr Sampson many years,' he said. I only knew him as David, a customer for many years at the Ship and the Travs. When I got in the box I noticed there were no police in attendance, when I questioned why I was told, 'You have pleaded guilty, they never attend.' I remembered Ronnie Teeman's words of knowing when to take advantage of a situation so I flowered the story of the bullying co-driver in the police car whilst remembering I was under oath. A minimum fine was once again imposed, together with the 12 month ban.

Our Malc's first born, Lee, had decided during the late 1980's to kick-start his career. Since the age of twelve he was an out and out winger and as in most junior grades, lack of involvement could prove frustrating, the odd pass finding its way across, or having to make or miss the occasional tackle. I believe that Lee became disillusioned with the game at this time and throughout his teens he opted out. However the lure of the game was too much and he returned to the fold once again as a winger for Stanley Rangers open age.

As a raw-boned youngster, he showed potential and I had the privilege of playing along side him in my 44th year, neither of us missed many games that season and subsequently when I took over the coaching reins at Doncaster I felt he justified my taking him along. He came up through the A-team and earned his spurs, Lee had exceptional pace and although one or two rough edges were in his make up, he more than made up with his enthusiasm and commitment. He earned the respect of players like Dean Carroll, Graham Idle and Kevin Rayne, alas two unfortunate injuries restricted the number of his appearances at a vital development time for him. He did however show tremendous tenacity and potential in overcoming setbacks and even after my departure from Doncaster, Lee went on to trial with Castleford, then sign for Hunslet where he again made first grade. As the years rolled by he returned to Stanley Rangers, playing for the team now coached by his cousin Dean. I will always contend that had Lee not missed those vital formative years, he too would have played at the highest level. However, after receiving a depressed fracture of the skull he now coaches with the open age at Stanley and is highly regarded.

27. Heartbreak Hotel

'Oh what a night, late December back in 63. What a very special night for me. I remember what a night.'

That song was on the jukebox as I left the Travs but I didn't realise I was heading for Heartbreak Hotel.

Well in my case it was late November 1989 and I was leaving my beloved Stanley village and heading for pastures new. Mavis and myself had been licensees for a solid 18 years in Stanley. I had been coaching at Doncaster since July and things were going quite well but the travelling between Stanley and Doncaster was tedious and time consuming. I felt I couldn't give my best to both so after hearing that I was looking for a pub in Doncaster one of the then directors of the club approached me and informed me that his, the Tadcaster Arms, was available so I agreed to take a look with Mavis.

It was a big animal but I could see it had potential. He stated he would take less with it being me and £25K was his bottom mark. I agreed and the pub company agreed. He informed me that 29th of November was the day he wanted to changeover and I went along with it, taking for granted he would inform the brewery as outing licensee.

When Mavis and I arrived, it was after 8 o'clock in the evening. The outgoing landlord asked if I had brought his money and I gave him £15K and explained I was late getting my cheque from Tetley's. 'I'll bank it tomorrow and then give you the balance.' I also gave him another £6K from Mavis' account but he seemed nervous and over keen to get his money in cash so I told him I would quickly clear the Tetley's cheque and pay him the remainder.

I was puzzled why no brewery rep was present at the handover but had been reassured that it was because I was late and they would be in touch. There were also several emergency lights not fitted and the lounge curtains were folded on a chair in a back room. I'd peeked into the other room and noticed some glass light shades stacked in the corner, 'What are these?' I asked.

'Oh they're the emergency ceiling light covers. The electrician has forgotten to fix them and with the decorator only just finished we haven't had time to put up the curtains or the shades.'

I did not want to make waves, it was late and we were tired. In normal circumstances, I would have said something but then he was a director of the club. 'What the hell,' I thought, 'I'm sure I can sort it later and pay his £4K balance the day after.' Little did I know what was about to unfurl or should I say unfold.

The curtains that were folded in a neat pile had been disturbed by Mavis. They were in shreds. Someone had neatly folded them after washing with none of the flaws showing. 'I can't hang these,' Mavis cried. 'We'll have to have new.' I quickly counted the windows, 'Good God' I thought, 'It's going to cost me an arm and a leg.' I recalled the curtains were in our agreement. I immediately smelled a rat, 'What about the lighting?' I thought.

Next day my electrician fitted all the lights and fittings and then those dreaded words, 'David can you come and look at this?' I followed the electrician down the cellar to where the emergency lighting power packs were situated.

'Oh my God!' They were furred up under the lids with what looked like two inches of snow.

'These haven't worked for a long time and it will cost a bob or two to fit new,' the electrician stated.

'Well,' I thought to myself, 'I still owe him £4,000. I'll talk to him first see if it can be sorted.' If I coughed up everything I'd be knackered, I knew that much. There seemed to be an unavoidable crisis arising. I'd only been in Doncaster a couple of days now and I'd almost been stitched up for over two grand, yes that's what it was going to cost.

The confrontation was next night at the ground. 'I'll knock you 500 quid off,' he snapped, 'It's not negotiable.'

'I'll give you the balance out of the £4,000 when I've got the curtains up and emergency lights done and paid for,' I replied.

End of my first week I was at loggerheads with a director and I'd had a fall out with a few customers in the taproom. It seems that what had been the norm for them was a mile apart from my standards. Drugs were rife and some customers were insolent, 'You're only here to serve us beer cock,' one had stated. Getting a please and thank you was unheard of by about fifty percent of them and yet the lounge side was as different again, lovely people. I'd pleaded to Mavis, 'Will you take taproom as yours love? You can't expect me to work in there they have no respect.'

My first Monday came and the brewery rep called in. He got a surprise when he saw me. 'What are you doing here?' he asked.

'I took over last Tuesday' I replied. 'Why, what's the problem.'

'But we don't know anything about it,' retorted the rep. 'I had better ring in to the office.' When he came back, he asked, 'Have you paid out any money?'

'Yes I have, £21K. What's the problem, I was late last week and assumed you couldn't wait? I was told everything was sorted.'

' No.' answered the rep. 'He owes us money and we would not have let him go without taking it out of the valuation.'

'Well I'm sorry, where do we go from here? I'm in court in the morning for my license.'

'Well you'd better go ahead and I'll try to sort it out.'

I attended court the next morning and who should be there but the outgoing tenant. When I went into the dock he stood up and objected to my application on the grounds I owed him money. The Magistrate told him to sit down and that was a matter for the Civil Court and not here. I was duly given my interim license and on the way out as I passed my objector, I put my face to his and quietly told him to come outside and sort it out, but not quite in those words.

The brewery rep came back to see me. 'Right David, what we can offer you is a one-year contract. That's all that's being offered at this moment in time.'

What they really meant is if we offer you a longer contract we shall want a lot more money. I replied, 'Let me find out first what power he wields at the rugby club.' I subsequently learned the Chairman was the sole power broker and the rest were just puppets.

Mavis worked hard to make a go of the pub. I occupied my time and energies out back building a beer garden. We had a patio and barbeque area and bought a horse for Becky, a goat and a donkey. The rugby was going well but I was far from settled.

One night I received a phone call at about 1 am from a so-called big hitter among the taproom hierarchy complaining that he wasn't happy about a certain member of staff and told me certain people might be interested that I was purchasing from other sources than I should be. I remember thinking, 'He's having a go because I've stopped big time gambling,' so I told him, 'I've just laid a lawn out back and fenced it off why don't you come straight over and we can sort it out?' He hung up.

A few weeks later my goat was savaged during the night but no sign of where a dog had got in or out. Another couple of weeks and we found the donkey dead. Then a further two weeks on, a brick through the window, followed by telephone threats to Mavis threatening to blow her legs off. This was coupled with problems I was having with the Chairman and the Dons Social Club so I told the brewery to get someone else for the pub.

I'd had enough. I couldn't fight cowards who come in the cover of darkness seeking to intimidate and threaten your family and livelihood. It was a glorious day when we finally left. The valuers agreed £15,000 so it had cost me financially. In retrospect I should have used a solicitor, had the place independently valued and an accountant to check the books. But then I hadn't expected to be tricked by a director of the rugby club that employed me. I suppose enthusiasm clouded my rationale.

It's unfortunate but in my opinion based on 30 years experience as a publican, the pub companies now are much like the breweries of old. They have outmanoeuvred successive governments to make a mockery of the so-called rights of the tenant. For example, if one of the so-called theme pubs moves in down the street, you quickly find they're able to undercut you given they're likely paying £100 less for a barrel of beer. And then your own company increases your rent but gives you a small discount on the beer you buy knowing you'll only sell a few barrels more whilst their rent is guaranteed. However, if you do buck the trend and make a large increase in sales, the next time they review your rent it's based on your successful efforts.

I don't know of an independent industry watchdog who will counsel prospective licensees, only of brewery sponsored courses which simply teach the basics in bookeeping, hygiene and cellar management. The odds are stacked against the licensee. If they are lucky and the marriage survives, the business survives and they remain healthy then I'm sure that their visits to Shangri-la will be numerous but there will not be many others of this chosen profession to compare notes with.

At Doncaster I was determined to give it my best shot despite the seemingly endless obstacles. The Chairman assured me that the previous coach, John Sheridan, who had recommended me, would be staying on as football director. I was perfectly happy with this arrangement and disappointed when the Chairman told me he had changed his mind. He would work with me as football director instead.

I wasn't sure how John would take this so I rang him and explained it was none of my doing and that I was happy to work with him. He replied, 'I am not surprised he's done a U-turn David. It's how he works.' I was to find that out for myself.

John made a return trip to the club after I left. I'm inclined to think he fell for some more blarney from the Chairman. I certainly did. Word had come from the secretary, Granville Bowen that my suggestion to sub-let the social club had been given the green light at a board meeting. I don't know if it really went before the board but I knew it was a way to introduce much needed funds. I arranged for a valuer and made an offer from a shelf company I held. To cut a long story short my company purchased the fixtures and fittings at the club and paid one month rent in advance, approximately £36K in total. I was then informed two weeks after taking over that the brewery had told the chairman that under no circumstances would a sub-lease be allowed and that it was quite clearly stated in the lease document. I learned from the brewery that they had informed the club of this by fax two days before my sub-lease deal had gone through but the Chairman had gone ahead with the changeover regardless, making the excuse to our valuers at the time that the legal papers were held up. We fell for it, my accountant and partner had been hoodwinked. The chairman had sold to us something he knew he did not have the right to sell. We demanded our money back but he said he'd spent the money by this time and could not return it. He came up with differing ideas to pay us back, constantly changing the goal posts, but in truth, I never received my £36,000 despite taking legal action and running up another £10,000 in costs. I was promised by him that on moving from the Tadcaster Arms. He would have the property adjoining the social club ready for me, another bit of blarney. I had swallowed the bait, hook, line and sinker.

Trying to coach and sort the mess with the social club bearing in mind we were unhappy at the Taddys Arms would have tested any coach's capabilities and I pushed myself to the limit as did Mavis. We simply did not deserve that man.

28. Benidorm, Drugs and Booze

An age old question, 'Do I have any experiences of drugs in rugby?' The answer would have to be yes and that's aside from knowing an oddball who liked four pints before a match. He was a brewery drayman, but I feel sure nowadays alcohol based supplement would be banned. The saying goes fatigue makes cowards of us all. If that's true then surely alcohol feeds bravado although this day and age with the speed of the game, four pints might come back to haunt a player in the middle of a match.

As for myself, I never knowingly took drugs but I do believe my Doctor once gave me a performance enhancing injection, two actually. He said, 'You have a urinary tract infection. I'll give you a jab and It'll be gone in a couple of days.' It was a Wednesday afternoon and I never thought about the game that evening. We were at Leigh. Arthur Keegan our player coach said to me after, 'David that's the best game I've ever seen you play. What have you been taking?'

'Oh thanks Arthur, their prop gave me a crack first scrum so I decided to show him who best man was.' It never crossed my mind that it might be the shot in either cheek at 4 o'clock but I considered it later.

But seriously anyone who has been involved with rugby if they are honest will tell you drugs have and do exist in the game. Personally I believe in the simplistic view that players should be allowed to use performance enhancing substances if they want but only if administered and monitored by doctors and that the players be educated as to the long-term harmful consequences. This would bring the whole issue out in the open and has to be better than cheating.

My personal experience came as quite a shock to me and it was after I had finished with the game at a professional level. My son Dean came home one day and said, 'JJ wants you to give him a ring Dad.' JJ was John Joyner the Cas coach at that time. I duly rang John. 'Now then mate, what can I do you for you?'

'Well it's a favour Sammy. I want you to take my place on the end of season trip to Benidorm. I can't make it and it won't cost you and I'll feel safe that there is somebody chaperoning my lads just so they don't go too far. Well you know what I mean, they respect you mate.'

'Mavis,' I yelled, 'Can I go to Benidorm on Wednesday with our Dean and the lads?'

'Of course you can.' came the reply.

'Game on.' I told John. He proceeded to give me all the details. Mini bus from Cas Bus Station to Humberside Airport, land at Alicante then taxis to the hotel and a top floor suite of rooms.

Everyone paired off when we arrived and I was last up the stairs. I was rooming with, well let's call him Peter. Although not as tall as me Pete was very very heavy set. He bounced on to the first bed CRASH! The bed broke. 'Oh fuck,' he said.

'That's yours for the week, drunk or sober,' I told him.

I had seen him on the plane and in the airport but I didn't recognise him as a player and we had not yet been introduced. I helped him up from the mattress and shook his hand. Further questioning brought out that he owned a gymnasium in Cas and he had like me filled the place of a player who couldn't make it. We then showered in turn and set off looking for the bright lights of Benidorm. It was a fair trek down and I had already made my mind up I would get a cab back. If I was going to keep up with this lot I'd have to conserve energy I thought, 'I've no problem keeping up with the drink but not with the energy factor.'

Well that first night I was introduced to new drinking games. I made a name for myself on the Karaoke, 'Randy Savage,' the DJ said after Tony Smith had said I was 'Randy Savage the Wrestler.'

The DJ remembered five years later when I sang 'House of the Rising Sun' it's a memorable song - eat your heart out Eric Burdin.

On the way back I staggered out of the taxi and made my way to the front doors I was just a few feet from the entrance and there was a WHOOSH and then another and then another. I jumped for cover under the canopy, I was soaking. On the floor were three plastic bags split open and a wet patch on the mezzanine tiles, I'd been water bombed. I caught the lift up to my floor fuming. 'They could have killed me if one had landed on my head.' I thought. When I left the lift everything was in darkness and all was quiet. I began thinking maybe it was from a lower balcony. Maybe my lads are still down town so I went to bed. I was woken by Martin Ketteridge and the others laughing and joking as they made their way back, Peter then started snoring in the next bed and I couldn't get back off. 'This is going to be a tough old week' I thought.

Early next morning I decided to walk to the shops to get myself a pair of flip-flops. I had nothing on my feet, just a T-shirt and shorts and sure enough before I reached the shops I trod on some glass and a piece embedded itself in my heel. It was painful as hell and I couldn't find it to get it out. I tried a Red Cross beach hut she pointed me to a chemist. The chemist pointed back to the beach hut, so I sat and waited for the lads. A few cups of coffee later they all emerged. Everyone denied any knowledge of the water bombs the previous night although I knew better. The sun was hot and the crack was good but I decided to go back to the digs, run a hot bath and see if I could find and remove this irksome piece of glass.

As I approached the front doors I looked skyward to the 13th floor. 'Nothing, must all be out.' I thought. They were, all except one. As I opened the door to our room, sat on the floor (furniture cleared to the side) was Peter and a mountain of capsules. It was 18 inches high and 2 feet across. He looked up.

'What the fuck is this?' I asked. 'What do you think you are doing?' I counted six hessian orange duffle bags strewn around the room and a pile of small empty boxes on the bed.

He calmly replied 'Stocking up.'

'For who and what exactly are they?' They were all the colours of the rainbow. One colour capsules, two-tone capsules. 'Peter,' I said, 'Are these what I think they are?'

'Yeah but its no big deal. It's legal to buy them over here.'

'It can't be legal to take them back to the UK I'm sure of that.' I said. My mind was racing ten to the dozen. I thought 'If he's caught, and with us there will be hell to pay. John Joyner would never forgive me.'

'What exactly are you doing with them Peter?' I asked.

'Well I make them up into saleable packs. These are for weight loss, burn off body fat. These are for muscle bulk. These are for...'

I interrupted him, 'So two of those one of those two of those make up a box of mixed drugs and are ready to sell?'

'Yes,' he said 'Right.'

I asked, 'Do any of our lads take them?'

'No chance,' he said. 'That's why they don't win owt.'

'Are you telling me you have customers who play rugby who do take them?'

'Oh yes.' he glibly replied and he proceeded to name clubs and players.

Of course I wouldn't name anyone because I don't have hard evidence and nor do I wish to anyway. It's just on this basis I hold the opinion like Wilf Paish the athletics coach, that there are some players and athletes who have slipped the net and are sporting trophies and awards achieved unfairly. Let's have it out in the open. That is my belief.

As for Pete, he continued making up these packs of drugs and feeding them into his suitcase which he'd brought over practically empty. I told him that he could not stay with us any longer and I wanted him out for the sake of the players and potential consequences his actions might bring on the team. After finishing packing he went and booked a flight home. Next morning he went back to England via Manchester not Hull where we embarked from. I heard later that his gym had closed and he was in Thailand. I don't think he's there for the sun.

As for the rest of the holiday, I had the time of my life. I never found the bombers but I have my suspicions and the lads were no trouble to anyone was my report back to John.

29. At Least It Wasn't December

I had left the Travs and moved over to Doncaster because John Desmond the chairman had convinced me that he personally would finance the building of a team to gain promotion. As related earlier, I had bought a pub from one of his co-directors, the Tadcaster Arms at Armthorpe but I was not a happy man during this period of my life.

I had moved from Stanley by Christmas 1989, then Mavis fell very ill, my daughter Becky's education was suffering and my son Jonathan who had never ever been in trouble had got himself locked up in Scotland. I was once again drinking heavily. I was unhappy in the pub in Doncaster and I was spending more and more time back in Stanley.

My ability at that time to consume alcohol for long periods and appear in control was legendary, still is for that matter but now it happens less often. Anyhow, it was approximately 2 am January 1st, 1991. It was the first New Year that I hadn't shared with my family. Mavis was at the Taddy and I was in Stanley then on to Methley. My good friend Tony Tighe had taken a pub in Methley village and it was on my way home. I often called and sang a couple of numbers for them accompanied by the resident organist.

I was driving back down the Motorway I had got December out of the way and I felt comfortable. My faculties seemed fine, I was approaching the M18. This would be my turn off and straight through to Armthorpe. I was cruising at 60, don't want to call attention to myself, seat belt on, lights dipped full beam when suddenly out of nowhere, cruising at 60 alongside me was a Motorway Police car and they were looking across at me, I noticed they were four handed. This went on for about half a mile. I looked across and nodded to the co-driver. They were all laughing and joking with each other and I thought they're pissed that's for sure but it's New Years Eve after all.

Live and let live.

This escort carried on for about another half mile. By this time I was getting pissed off with them so I powered my window down. The co-driver did the same. 'Is there a problem officer?' I yelled.

'Only for you.' came the sarcastic reply. 'Pull over, we want a word.'

I was going to pit all my breathalysing experience against those arrogant baskets, well, against three of them, the fourth, the driver, he probably saved my bacon as I later realised.

'Where have you been Sir?'

'Stanley and Methley Officer.' I answered.

'And where are you going Sir?'

'Armthorpe Officer.'

'Where do you live in Armthorpe Sir?'

'Tadcaster Arms Officer.'

'Oh a publican eh?' One of the others chimed in.

'The pub has many rooms, because I live there does not automatically make me the landlord. However in this case yes I am a publican and the landlord, son.'

'Oh a clever bastard have we as well?' another chimed in.

'If anyone's questioning anyone's parentage, well there are four of you and one of me. That puts odds in your favour. Anyway how do I know your not impostors who have been to a fancy dress party?'

One of them said, 'We have reason to believe you have been drinking Sir. Would you please step out of the car.' Then turning to the others who were agitated by now. 'The rest of you calm down.'

Two of them immediately grabbed on each arm and escorted me to the nearside. I did not offer any resistance. 'Spread your legs and face the car asshole.' said one. 'I'll check him.' said the other.

I turned my head to the driver, 'Officer isn't the procedure to take me to your car and ask me to give you a breath sample or are these morons playing cops and robbers because it's the festive season?'

I had no sooner got the words out when a hand went between my legs and grabbed my testicles. I think I shouted. It was agonising. I was on my tiptoes gritting my teeth and feeling nausea coming on.

'Let him go,' shouted the driver, 'From now on it's by the book.' but it was too late.

The policeman who'd grabbed my balls stood back a pace. His two mates had released my arms and I turned to face him. The pain was excruciating. 'Spoiled a good arse when they put teeth in your mouth.' I snarled at him to wipe the big grin off his face. He stepped forward, just what I wanted. With the flat of both hands I hit either shoulder. He staggered back one pace too many. His legs hit the barrier and down the embankment he went. His legs were the last thing I saw as he disappeared into the darkness. The driver grabbed me as did the other two. I then protested, 'Take me in now or else let's get it on.' They looked at each other.

'Go down and get him,' snapped the driver. 'Into the car you.' He shouted at the one going down the bank, 'Bring his car back to the station.'

I was bundled into the back of the police car and we sped off. 'Now then driver you are supposed to ask me which station I would like to attend in order to take a blood test. Also as of yet you have failed to ask me to take a breath test on the roadside in order to confirm your suspicions. You've fucked up big style I'll tell you.' I then kept quiet.

I was presented to the desk sergeant. He recognised my name instantly. 'Don's coach aren't you?'

'Yes' I replied. 'I wish to exercise my legal right to speak to a duty solicitor. I will not take a breath test of any description. I am in violation of a traffic offence and unless other charges are going to be pressed, I would like you get me a taxi home and I will send a driver for my car in the morning. It's New Years Day and my wife will be worried where I am.'

'Constable lock Mr Sampson in cell number two while I sort this out.'

Then just as I was going through the door into the cells, in came the other two policemen. The one I had pushed came straight to open the door. 'I'll have you that's a promise.' He was crimson faced and the others held him back. I could not resist. 'Hey Sarge, lock him in with me for an hour. He'll come out humbler than he went in.'

The door closed on me. I wasn't happy but I'd stood my ground. I never intended taking the breathalyser. I was prepared to take my punishment drunk or sober but not my civil liberties and dignity taken away. A few minutes later the key turned in the lock. 'Follow me Sir.' When I got back the phone was off the hook, the sergeant said 'It's for you.'

It was the duty solicitor, I repeated that it was a traffic offence and I wanted out unless I was being charged and yes, I had refused to co-operate by taking a breath test. He asked me to pass the phone to the Sergeant. Ten seconds later the Sergeant was on the phone. 'Can I have a taxi for Mr Sampson to go to the Tadcaster Arms, Armthorpe please? Yes straight away.'

The Sergeant escorted me to the door. 'What happened back there when you were pulled?' he asked.

'Nowt.' I replied, 'Unless they tell you any different.'

'Well they've had a confab and just reported that you refused a breath test which I can concur.'

'Then that's what it will be.' I added.

Arriving home I got a rollicking off Mavis. After a while she came round but my privates were sore for days. The court case was at Howden Court a little hamlet between Goole and Selby. Nice and quiet I thought as I arrived July 7th, 1991. I had managed to get it adjourned because I was moving back to Stanley and I did not mind a ban as long as I was home. The fact the court was quiet suited me too. No press I was hoping and I was right. Well I'd pleaded guilty there were no police officers in attendance and I told it as it was. The chief magistrate was a real old salt, a Hull Kingston Rovers supporter. He was just about to dismiss the case when the registrar asked him to retire into the back chamber. He came back out and said the following. 'Well Mr Sampson. I was going to dismiss the case but I'm informed that you have pleaded guilty and give you the statutory three years ban for a second offence. However, I can tell you that I am ordering the minimum fine in this case of £300 and I am unhappy that I can't do more for you. I wish you well.'

I left the Court feeling neither elated nor deflated, just resigned. I'd done the crime now do the time. I did three years ban to July 1994. I then decided I would self impose another year to make sure that I was in absolute control.

30. I Believed the Blarney

After leaving the Taddy Arms and investing the money received into the Social Club renovations, we moved into a little bungalow in Pontefract. This was rented from Harrison's of Castleford initially for Taime Tagaloa, a New Zealander we had signed. He had arrived injured and had been sent home. The chairman, John Desmond said he would pay the rent for me until I could move into the Social Club. Our Rebecca slept on the settee, Jonty in the other bedroom, Mavis and I in the main bedroom. It was small but it was a roof over our heads. Mavis was running the social club and commuting to Doncaster while I was running the rugby but my wages were not being paid by the club so Mavis was the sole provider. I felt that a hole was being dug for us and it was getting deeper.

The chairman was full of empty promises so we decided to purchase Stanley Working Men's Club in my old village and plan my future elsewhere. I insisted to him, 'I want my money or at least half of it now or I'm going to sue.' He gave me a cheque for £20K but it bounced then he replaced it with a cheque for £15K and this bounced first time of asking but then went through. Dean added three grand and we paid the deposit on the Working Men's Club. We had a completion date of September 7th, 1991 and the chairman had given me his word I would get the balance of my money in time. The brewery had offered a £150K mortgage but three days before completion and nothing from the chairman then the brewery rep called to inform me that the offer had failed to get board approval. I was furious. I talked to the top people at the brewery then one of the directors rang me, 'I've got you £135K David. Best I can do.'

'I'll take it.' I snapped. 'If I don't complete then my deposit is forfeit. We've nowhere to live and we will be on the street.'

I explained the situation to Dean. He came back several hours later with £15,000. That's the kind of man he had grown into, I recall thinking there was a lot of grandad in him. However, little did we know we were moving into the belly of a whale, its appetite never satisfied.

Harrison's had taken the bungalow back because the chairman had not paid any rent from day one. Mr Harrison had been good when I'd explained my predicament and let us stay just long enough to move into the Stanley Club.

I finished up with the sack at Doncaster by telephone and the remaining money paid out for renovations in the social club was never paid back although I did get my rugby wages on the court steps, metaphorically speaking. The chairman played stalling tactics and changed solicitors. My solicitor Robert Brown advised, 'Walk away David, he will continue to lead you a merry dance, you're throwing good money after bad.'

I was so incensed at the injustice of it all that I went to the following year's shareholders meeting. The first for four years and at the request of some other shareholders, they too suspected my allegations were well founded and together with their own complaints a strategy was planned. I would attend by proxy and fire my questions from the floor. On examination of the accounts I could see my introduction of £36,000 did not exist. It simply was not shown anywhere. I questioned this to the auditors on stage. 'Why is there no mention of £36,000 being introduced by my company? I have a copy of the cheque in my possession and a letter and bank statement proving it was paid to Doncaster RLFC. I repeat why is it not shown?'

The chairman and his new auditors had a quick whisper to each other, 'Well Mr Sampson, we had to pay some accounts so we contra'd one against the other.'

'But you show these accounts being paid as outgoings, that's obvious to anyone who can read a set of accounts. Why do you not show the £36,000 income? The club received this money tell us why it is not shown?'

At this the chairman interceded, hey you did all right out of it David at which many of his well placed cronies began heckling and the Chair proceeded.

I was livid with this man, he had temerity to make that statement after all his false promises indicating I had come out of it all right. He had almost left my family and me on the street. He got the vote at the meeting by one vote but I later found out that the consortium containing some major shareholders had been refused entry. They were informed that the meeting had started and they were too late.

He was as slippery as an eel.

I later received a visit from the VAT office. Two senior Inspectors. I was interviewed at length and exonerated of VAT liabilities regarding the social club but their parting shot was, 'We have not finished with the club and the chairman Mr Sampson.'

The rugby team gained promotion to the premier division and did exceptionally well under Tony Fisher the new coach but it was to be short lived. The chairman's bubble burst. He may have come out of it okay but alas the club have been like gypsies over the past few years moving from ground to ground and I understand once again are in financial difficulties. It is hoped their demise does not follow the path of dear old Bramley so soon after basking in glory. The last time I spoke to Tony Fisher he was no longer employed by the club and said he was £15K adrift. I wonder what percentage of coaches and players have been financially stung or had to work under such distressing and distracting pressures? Not many I hope for I would not wish it on anyone. The chairman had manipulated everyone.

There are many loyal and fine people who support the Dons. Hopefully the club will pull through the difficult legacy of that time and maybe soon Super League rugby will someday come back to South Yorkshire.

I understand the chairman lives somewhere in Ireland. I hope it pisses it down every day just to remind him that what goes around comes around. I never got my day in court but I did manage to survive this episode by the skin of my teeth returning to my beloved village of Stanley ready to take up the challenge that Samson's Free House was to offer.

31. One Fine Day Made Our Summer

After Doncaster and the disgraceful way I felt my family had been dealt with, coaching again was the last thing on my mind. But then my old friend and stalwart Graham Idle called for a drink in Samson's to sound me out about taking on the job at Nottingham. Now Graham was very persuasive, 'Only one way they can go, you'll have full control. The chairman would like to meet you.' Graham was also up for 25 years as a professional player. A marvellous achievement. I'd played with him at Bramley when he started as a young full back and he like myself had adapted to play in the pack. He had rejoined me at Doncaster and had been first man on the team sheet every week, his work rate was still colossal and younger players respected him for he was one of the most positive player's I have ever known.

I met the chairman of Nottingham at a motel on the M1. He impressed me enough to convince me to take a look at the stadium a couple of days later. The Harvey Hadden Stadium and Sports Centre was impressive, I finalised things with the chairman based on the promises that were made and so I took up the challenge.

First job I contacted Trevor Briggs. Trev had been my assistant at Doncaster where we had made a formidable team. He was very capable, impeccably honest and loyal and a friend to boot, we also had played together at Bramley. But bringing Trevor on board was the easy part as he was ultra keen to get back into the game. Trying to get players was much more difficult. I tried to contact most of the players who were registered with the club but several said they were owed money and wouldn't come back and others had packed in. All in all, I didn't have a team or any money to buy one, this was turning into a mountain of a job.

Trevor came up trumps with somewhere to train. Rothwell Grammar School, we would use it three times per week. First recruit apart from Graham Idle was Lee my brother Malc's boy. Lee was a solid defender and could play centre or wing, he would cope fine at this level. I recruited Craig McEllhatton on loan from Wakefield. He could play half back or hooker. Each week we were adding new faces. Neil Clawson, Featherstone's second row at open side prop, Dick Fairbanks from Halifax. I'd written to two Aussies who were paying their own fare over. Brad Davis and Jason Lawrence. Both were to go on to Super League standard. Three or four lads started coming up from Nottingham. A J Okiwe, a winger who had played with Sheffield. Tony James, a winger from Huddersfield, Paul McDermot a utility vet at loose forward and Nick Grimalby, a good second rower with plenty of enthusiasm. It was taking shape and Trev and I were starting to feel comfortable.

I had purchased some new tackle bags and shields as the kit that the chairman had supplied us was soiled and unacceptable. I slipped the lads a few quid expenses each to keep the smiles on their faces. David Holmes a former England B Rugby Union scrum half joined us. He had been with me at Doncaster but then suffered an injury to his knee so he was back to try again, as was young Brian McDermott who joined us from Eastmoor and later went on to Bradford.

It was time to take a look at them as a team so I organised a friendly match against Leeds to be played at Bramley. My old club co-operated and somehow we had television cameras in the dressing rooms. Our Dean and Jonathan sold programmes on the gate as entrance fee and Leeds paid me a compliment by fielding a strong team. We lost the match but Trevor and I saw enough to build on. We knew a win was just around the corner.

Now Nottingham was not a place filled with rugby league fans but all the lads attended a promotion day in the town centre. I had purchased a new all green strip with a Robin Hood style archer as an emblem and we named ourselves the Outlaws. The money and time I had spent to date was beginning to mount and because of my Doncaster experience I didn't want to go too far out on a limb before the club coughed something up. The chairman and his mother were insistent that the money, about 1,800 quid, for the Leeds game was handed over which I reluctantly did but we needed regular bus transport. When I contacted Clive Bowie who I had known for some years he said he had been the coach driver for the previous two years but the club owed him £80 so until he got it, no buses. I asked him for a price he said 100 quid same as last year. I said make it £120 for the first four trips and that way I get a bus and you get your 80 quid. He agreed.

In our first game against Blackpool, we went down narrowly. It was tipped that they would be the top team that year so we were not too unhappy. Many individual performances in the side were giving us encouragement but we needed more time to develop as a unit. The following week would be a test for us with the long trip to Barrow so we worked hard in training, the atmosphere was terrific.

It was a lovely September day when the lads trotted out. Barrow were expecting to win easily and there were about 1,500 fans who also thought the same but our lads had decided differently. Now at this moment as the teams kicked off, Nottingham Rugby League Club had not won any of the previous 42 games - almost two years without a victory. Now my coaching record with the Cas A-team, the first team and at Doncaster stood at over 75% and this day ranked among the top five in my career. We won the game, the first in 42 and their last as a professional club. Every player had been literally written off by other clubs as surplus to requirements but on this historic day everyone played their part, Trevor and myself, all the players and even the rubber downer, Griss Ansell. Barrow were absolutely devastated but like true pros, very gracious and hospitable and we milked it. All the team were milling about having something to drink and eat when at last I caught the chairman's eye. He was stood with his mother who I had long suspected as being the real governor. I made my way across expecting to receive some congratulatory remark when Mrs Tomlinson spoke very curtly and direct. 'We were just discussing, we have Chorley as our next home game in two weeks. Do you think we will win that?'

'Yes I do.' I replied. 'And York had better watch out at home the week after because this is all we needed, a confidence boost and a mixture of youth and experience all pulling the same way.'

'But that's not good enough. We have not budgeted for winning pay. Another week and we can't pay the wages!'

I was gob smacked. So far since I'd joined they had paid two lots of losing pay, a few hundred pounds and I'd invested about £10K if you include £3,000 for three months wages. Tomlinson had told me they were financially secure but I'd obviously been lied to once again. I turned to walk away then I half turned back, 'If you can't stand the heat get out of the kitchen.' I was utterly disillusioned and I broke the news to Trevor. 'Don't tell the lads.' I asked, 'Let them have their day.' A few days later Mr Tomlinson rang to tell me, 'We can't afford these two Aussies. Send them home and the players on loan send them back. You'll have to field a team of locals.'

Well I didn't feel like starting all over again so I broke the news to everyone and put my bill in for expenses and wages to date. Unfortunately I had to sue for those and it was Maurice Lindsay who I had sent a report to who advised, 'Wind them up David. They are like leeches in the game.'

I reluctantly told the media my story and issued a winding up order. Mr Tomlinson went on to reply that I had pushed up transport costs by eighteen percent in my first month and that I was a Greek bearing fits. I never bothered to reply. I knew the truth and as at Doncaster I had been stitched up. In the real world how the hell did they expect us to build a side from nothing on nothing. I was good at my job but not that good.

I was never to coach professionally again but my spirit was only dented. They could not break my love of the game no matter how hard they tried.

Some time later my good friend Trevor was killed in a fatal road accident. He had been on his way back from Workington after watching his son Carl play and was, like every Sunday, heading back for a drink with me at Samson's. He is sadly missed but I still have those wonderful memories.

As for Nottingham, they died also as a professional club and that was also sad. People like the Desmond's and the Tomlinson's of this world were not steeped in Rugby League, its traditions and values like myself, Trevor Briggs or Graham Idle. They don't understand that the hard graft isn't for the money or that the players demanded so little for plying their trade only to be used and abused and treat so contemptuously. Personally I think they were only in the game to make a quick buck and that players and fans were only a means to an end. Surely somehow we should be able to put in place administrative powers to uphold the dignity our wonderful game deserves for I know personally that abuse went on in the 1950's, 60's, 70's, 80's, and 90's. We cannot allow our game to be administered with the callous calculating apathy of our forbearers employers, and I ask that if plans are afoot regarding rugby and its planned future then let the people know.

32. In the Belly of a Whale

The early days at Samson's were tough. There was apathy by local club customers which is why it had come on the market in the first place. The mines were closing and many families were moving to the Selby Coalfield area. It is no co-incidence that from 1985 on, the Victoria Club, Bottomboat Club, Lee Moor Club and Stanley Lane Ends Club all closed, three of which went into private hands. In my case Stanley Lane End became Samson's without the 'P'. To quote Garth Archer, my rep at that time, 'You're the only one to take the P out of Samson's.'

The first 18 months were very difficult. I had retained Roy, the previous club steward as my bar and cellar manager. Roy was a long time friend and a former miner and rugby player. We discussed many ways of improving things and then we started to turn around this greedy giant.

Alas I was to lose Roy to cancer just a few short weeks after diagnosis. He had spent 19 years serving an ever-diminishing market only to be forced to serve another long before his time.

Samson's started doing well, the trade picked up and we became one of the top venues in the area but entertainment was still costly and it restricted the profit margins.

It was about this time Dean took up a contract to play for Parramatta in the land of Oz and he also had a loyalty bonus payment due from Super League. Dean faxed me from Australia and asked that I contact his bank and request a £5,000 loan whilst he waited for the Super League cheque so he could bring his wife and daughter and his mum and sister across to stay with him for a few weeks, however the bank refused. On hearing this my solicitor recommended another bank and they were prepared to lend Dean the money so I transferred the business account also.

That was one of the bad decisions of my life, I was unaware when putting our trust in them that the then bank manager had already foreclosed on my brother Brian, selling his pub from under him to another customer within the bank for £5K less than Brian had paid and Brian had spent £100K on restoring it.

It was in casual conversation with the manager, 'Are you related to Brian Sampson?' he had asked

'Yes he's my older brother why?'

'I just had not connected you together, him being over in Halifax you see.'

When I rang Brian and asked if this man meant anything to him, our kid hit the roof. 'He's a right so and so David. Don't get into bed with him and his bank. They are ruthless.'

Too late was the cry but Dean and I found his words proved very true. We found them worlds apart from any of the other financial houses we have dealt with. Three consecutive aggressive bullying bad mannered managers on the trot who gave you the impression you are an unwanted burden if in trouble and to be penalised whenever possible. We left them and moved to another bank that was recommended by our accountants. We found them accommodating and helpful and our manager, John Davies, gave us our self-esteem back and said that the bank accounts I had brought with us were bordering on the illegal.

We as a family will be eternally grateful to John, he helped us out of many a scrape and then supported us in building the business. However, when the Bank was taken over by another, John moved into a different role.

It took a while to establish Samson's but we did and had some heady days. Like the Ship a decade earlier, it became the local area Mecca and was the place for popular local bands such as the Muldoon Brothers. The customers would erupt within seconds, dancing, climbing on the chairs and this would go on for two hours, none stop. The Solicitors were another local band and the Daw Green Stompers, the list went on and on. Different music but all equally popular, full house, sold out, this happened often. We hosted the Northern Startrail talent show plus amateur boxing, thai boxing, and kick boxing, all to audiences topping 300 and never any security needed. I handled the door and in time everyone knew everyone else. All were fanatical fans of each show or sport but they had respect for where they were appearing, well, most of them did.

There are certain customers who can behave differently after alcohol but I believe if you have sold drink to them, tolerance is the best method with a little humour thrown in. There were odd occasions when it didn't work for me but I've only ever rung for the police once in 30 years so I must have been doing something right.

33. Shoe on the Other Foot

It was July 1995 and I bought a Jag confident that all would be well. I wrote off to the DVLA asking for my licence back. I got the car insured through my agent and paid £1000 cash for the insurance cover note. The documents came through a couple of days later. D Sampson insured party.

A friend of mine, John Hall, who ran the White Rose Boxing Club suggested we went to the Multi Nations Boxing Tournament in Liverpool and possibly stay in Blackpool and make a weekend of it. 'Yeah fine. We'll go in my car,' which we did. Another pal and member of White Rose, Paul Kelly accompanied us. Paul was an ex boxer of high quality and he was also a police officer. We booked in Blackpool at Gary Connell's Walford Hotel. Gary had played rugby with me at Cas in the early 1980's. It was Friday night and we had a little drink then went to bed. I drove from Blackpool next day to Liverpool. I drank four bottles of Volvic water all day, I was being a responsible citizen and it made me feel good. Anyhow, after the boxing I drove back to Blackpool. I pulled into Albert Road and was about 50 yards from the car park when guess what? Alongside me from nowhere pulled a police car. Just one lady driver. I turned and joked to John, 'This is one time I'll take a breath test.' She asked me to get into her car, pretty little thing she was.

'Is it your car?'

'Yes.' I replied.

'Will you take a breath test?'

'Sure I will, in fact I insist.'

'Why,' she queried 'Have you not had a drink?'

'No I haven't, why did you pull me?'

'Well you had your fog light on.'

Just then my mate Paul opened the car door, flashed his badge and said 'I've been with him all day. He's not had one drink.'

'OK,' she said. 'But I've started making out a producer so I'll have to give him it and make sure you know what lights you have on in future.'

Now the saga of this producer is about to unravel.

Monday morning I arrived in my office and explained what had happened to the girls. I asked them to contact DVLA regarding my licence requesting that they send it through immediately because I only had seven days to produce it. Christine my secretary pulled out my insurance documents and test certificate and so I relaxed that week, never imagining the problems about to unfold.

Come Friday I opened the post but nothing from DVLA so I trundled into Wakefield Police Station knowing my seven days were about to expire. Firstly, I explained what had happened and requested an extension of my producer. 'No chance,' snapped the desk officer. He logged the other two documents and sent me on my way.

Well I thought it will only be a small fine for not producing my licence on time. I'll produce it later, or that's what I thought.

You can imagine my glee on the Monday morning when the post arrived. An envelope clearly marked DVLA, I opened it and read the contents.

'Dear Mr Sampson due to the fact that you are now over 50 and having served a second ban you are now required by law to take and pass a medical examination before we can issue you with a driving licence...under no circumstances will your own doctor be allowed to do this medical.'

I rang the Surgery that the DVLA had nominated. 'Sorry Sir can't fit you in for another three weeks.' So be it I thought.

When I arrived and met the doc he was standing with his back to me looking out of the window. 'Just checking my new car's OK. It's that silver Volvo. Young kids around here you have to keep an eye on things. Right then Mr Sampson lets get on with it. You certainly look healthy enough. First of all we'll do your eyes. Can you stand on this line, put one hand over your left eye and read the letters on the wall?'

I proceeded to read them backwards starting with the smallest.

'Good God,' he exclaimed. 'OK stop. Try with the other.'

I proceeded to do the same.

'That's enough,' he drawled. 'Right step on these scales.'

I did. The needle quivered.

'14st 9lbs' stated the doc.

14st 9lbs I thought. I took a good look it was showing 17st 9lbs which was more like it. 'Are you sure doctor?' I questioned.

He took a closer look slightly bending and adjusting his glasses. '14.9 or 14.10 it doesn't need to be exact.'

With those words I stepped off the scales. If he was happy so was I. He then did my height which was six feet. Now that's the nearest I had been to the chart height to weight ratio for 25 years. After concluding my medical I thought to myself I hope he won't offer me a lift with eyesight like that!

Well it took another three weeks for the medical results to come through. I failed was the disappointing result. My liver reading was too high indicating that I was still drinking, well that was no secret but I never drank and drove. I then took advice from my own doctor and he was quite categoric. 'Stop drinking for three months,' which I duly did. He sent me for a blood test. 'Another three months,' came his reply which I also did. During this time I had received a summons to appear in Blackpool Magistrates Court to face prosecution of not producing my driving licence within the prescribed seven days. It was an early morning hearing so I travelled over the night before, ate out but no booze!

On standing in the dock the three magistrates listened intently to my story but then the Clerk of the Court came out with the bomb-shell. 'Your Worships,' he blurted. 'If Mr Sampson has not and cannot produce a driving licence then his insurance by law becomes invalid.' Now I immediately realised the implications were much more serious. I thought I've tried to do it by the book and I'm in the shit more than ever and all over a bloody fog light. I asked for an adjournment on advice from the magistrates which was duly granted.

On achieving six months without a drink I attended my own doctors expecting the all clear and a letter to apply for a driving licence. I was in for a shock. 'Sorry David your reading is still too high although it has improved significantly. Another three months should do the trick so don't give up.'

I was back in Blackpool the following day for my second hearing.

Now I thought I had a master card, the insurance company had given me a letter saying that I was insured at the time of driving and therefore my premium was not refundable unless I was permanently cancelling my insurance. Well on producing the letter in court, the clerk was quite dismissive. 'I must inform your Worships no matter what the insurance company say the law is quite clear on the matter. A person cannot obtain insurance without producing his or her driving licence. Mr Sampson admits to not having one. The DVLA will not return him one and therefore he is guilty on both counts.'

The Magistrate took a deep breath and spoke very slowly. 'Look Mr Sampson, if I were you I would take this case to a solicitor and fight it.'

'Your Honour,' I interjected. 'Please try the case as it stands, if I tell the wife I'm coming to Blackpool again she'll accuse me of having another woman. That would be the fourth trip.'

'Well if you insist,' he replied.

They retired and came back within minutes. 'Well Mr Sampson, we have taken into account what you have stated and we fine you the minimum £60 for driving without a licence, £40 for not producing your licence and the sum of £400 for driving without insurance, a figure that could have been substantially more notwithstanding the circumstances.'

I came out relieved it was over at last but if you add expenses and the fact that the insurance company insisted I was still insured then it was a bitter pill to swallow. As for abstaining, I did another three months making nine in all. This time the doctor said, 'You're nearly clear. Do another three months and I'll write and get you your licence back.'

'How long do I get my licence for?' I asked.

'Well six months then another blood test and if you're clear you get one for 12 months.'

I realised it was a straight choice. Stop drinking forever and be able to drive or have a sensible drink now and then and forget the driving. I chose the latter. I do not see myself as weak, I'm not an alcoholic but if I had been pulled and blood tested, my doctor said they would throw the book at me. I find this very difficult to accept but I suppose the law is there to protect road users. I just feel that even with the many many thousands of miles I have driven and never been pulled, except for suspicion, the decision to allow someone back on the road should be appraised in a different fashion than the random way it is. Perhaps a retest and automatic prison sentence for say, a third offence within a certain period of time. I'm not sure but a guy can be the driver in an armed robbery and he pays his debt to society. They do not take his driving licence away when he comes out never to return it to him because he is deemed untrustworthy or might re-offend.

34. A Wasp and a Wild Cat

When I received a call from my brother Brian asking me to discuss his son Paul's future with Nigel Melville at Woodhouse Grove School, I duly agreed. Apparently Nigel was uprooting himself to take up the post of director of rugby at Wasps rugby union club. A massive change of track from his teaching post and he wanted to take Paul along with him. Brian had no objections but because of his good friendship with Nigel and my experience of negotiating for Dean, he thought it better if I sort the business issues.

Nigel was a pleasure to do business with and we were all happy with the terms. Paul would be leaving school aged 18 and moving to London with a car, accommodation and a college place together with a sign on fee, monthly retainer, match terms and most of all, incentive increases on gaining honours. This was to prove a lucrative clause for Paul because he was later selected for England at both A-team and full levels in his first year, making him probably one of the best paid young guns in the game. However, as he started to reap the financial rewards and honours I had a feeling they were outstripping his development and experience. Now don't get me wrong, Paul has always been an impressive trainer, you couldn't win the All England Schools 100m title in 10.48 and just shading the likes of Dwaine Chambers without years of hard work, but what concerned me was the actual games he played were intermittent. Niggling injuries and inconsistent form meant a rethink might be necessary. All said, he was young and there was no need for panic.

Brian and myself often discussed his development and our thinking was he had left school and moved into a world of grown men 200 miles from a stable home and into an environment and lifestyle that would distract even the most dedicated of athletes.

When Paul signed a new two-year contract Brian and his mum, Christine, gave Paul advice on his lifestyle, managing his finances and his responsibilities to fulfil the faith other people had invested in him.

However, Brian was suffering from cancer at that time and whilst he had shown a resilience that belied his stature, I'm sure it was proving a further distraction to Paul given the close relationship they both had, let alone the limitations placed on Brian to motivate and coach his son. I particularly remember seeing Brian on TV with Paul. It was Kilroy the subject, 'Do we live our lives through our children?' Brian was forceful in stating, 'Yes I am using Paul to fulfil my dreams but only because I recognise his talent and Paul with my help and drive will realise his dream so it is a joint effort.' Paul enthusiastically concurred.

I remembered back to when we were younger, Brian was a good rugby player but not good enough to make it professionally. However, Brian was a brilliant artist. He attended college on leaving school only to marry at the tender age of 17 and took the path dad had insisted that none of us should follow, that of a miner. Brian endured the mines for 19 years, at times rebelliously and that didn't surprise me for a budding artist hewing coal and especially working with our dad must have been as soul destroying as it was character building. But Brian had done excellent job with Paul and steadily his off field activities were slowly turning around.

Alas Paul's frustration at not being able to secure a permanent place in the Wasps team was constantly rearing its ugly head. So we thought about it and decided a move might do him good or even a loan spell with Saracens. I suggested he might change codes and hinted a few Super League clubs were monitoring him. I then rang Nigel Melville and after a prolonged discussion we decided the terms of Paul's release, no fee but for Wasps to retain first option should he return to rugby union. Nigel quite sensibly had not given up hope on Paul and merely looked on the move as therapeutic.

35. They Saw Me Coming

The train was the 9.18 Leeds to London. I was on board with Andy Kelly, the Wakefield Trinity Wildcats coach and John Pearman the chief executive. We were travelling to the capital to meet my nephew Paul who at this time was contracted to Wasps rugby union club.

Paul had indicated if I could arrange a satisfactory deal he might change codes and my brother Brian and I were convinced that a couple of seasons in Super League would make him the finished article. I brokered the deal on the journey down to London and then over a couple of hours with Paul in the Great Northern Hotel. I had known Andy Kelly for many years and I was confident he would give Paul every assistance and although I did not know John Pearman I found him to be a very affable and business like gentleman. He had bartered that some of the monies Paul was to be paid would be match related and this included an extra lump sum of £5,000 on achieving 15 games and a further £5,000 if chosen for England.

Wigan, Warrington, St Helens, Castleford, and Wakefield were all clubs who had shown varying degrees of interest in Paul but Wakefield got the nod. His signing was carried out with a blaze of publicity and Paul moved north and knuckled down to training.

My work complete I concentrated on finishing the nightclub project I'd begun in Dewsbury. Then a couple of weeks later I received a call from Richard Kelly, Andy's brother who was the commercial manager at Wakefield. 'Would I be interested in meeting them for talks regarding the bars in the new hospitality complex?'

This approach could only have been triggered by casual small talk with John Pearman on that train journey. I recall thinking no harm would come from having a meeting, or at least I thought not. My son Dean was very much against any involvement and professed caution. He reminded me of the Doncaster and Nottingham experiences but I felt because of Paul's two-year contract, the club would behave in an honourable manner, so I attended the meeting.

The club offered me the contract for setting up the hospitality in the new £1 million stand but I had only a few weeks to carry out the task. I decided to take on the challenge and we opened on time only to find out that on completion Wakefield were unable to pay for the work. As a result, this effected my own business my company's cash flow was hit hard and I remember thinking Dean had been right and I had been wrong.

Wakefield's financial difficulties that season have been well documented elsewhere but the impacts on our own family were Paul's return to rugby union and the start of the demise of my own business. But I think what distressed me most was the negative press Paul received from the rugby union media which contained plenty of snide remarks as to why he was such a failure in contrast to the actual facts. It was also disconcerting that some of the rugby league media were equally negative by trying to make political gain in favour of a fictitious war between the two codes. I understand that they're trying to sell newspapers but this is sport. Both codes are full of athletes, coaches, administrators and fans who are simply fed up with some of the drivel being written, instead their editors should instruct them to use the space for informed facts, not unsubstantiated rumour and innuendo.

Anyway, Paul rejoined Wasps and was then chosen to tour North America with England and also scored two tries against the Barbarians. Praise is due to Nigel Melville for keeping faith with Paul whilst making him earn the right to a place in the team and to his mum and Dad for their immoveable support and encouragement and especially to Paul for maintaining a family tradition. His grandad George would have been so proud of him too.

Paul was on Sky TV recently for England v Canada. He limped from the field with a leg injury. Dean was also on Sky playing for Cas against Hull. He also limped from the field. He too a leg injury. The resultant news Paul a couple of months lay-off, Dean a couple of weeks. 'It all adds character,' dad would have proffered, 'Keep your spirits up.'

Next day we received news that Josh, Brian's grandson from his first marriage to Eileen had been chosen for an elite training squad for the north at rugby union. The conveyor belt continues.

Regarding my own business, well, things had been moving along nicely. Alongside Samson's we had acquired the Railway at Pontefract, the Houghton at Castleford and Barristers pub in Wakefield and we then had started with the nightclub but the Wakefield Trinity fiasco put us in a difficult situation with our finances. Unfortunately the management team in the nightclub were not generating the trade we expected and it was loosing around £4,000 a week.

We then decided to sell-off the Railway and secured a buyer but we were then advised (spuriously as it turned out) that our finance agreement on the Railway did not allow us to sell the pub until we had completely paid for it. This put us in deep shit. We suddenly owed the brewery a good deal of money without the means to pay. We offloaded the Barristers and the Houghton and this covered most of the debt but we still owed the brewery £15K. Now this might seem a lot of money but when you consider we had done over £650K trade with the brewery in the previous 12 months, well I guess that puts things into context.

Anyway, the brewery decided to start bankruptcy proceedings but we managed to get them to postpone when we were able to pay off £2,000 and then a further £4,000 soon after. Now after paying £6,000 I guess like me, most people would assume they had paid off nearly half the debt but then the brewery issued a bill for practically the same amount, £15,000 'Interest and charges David.' the brewery explained.

I was finding this game tougher than any I'd played before. If only I could have got their recoveries manager into a scrum I think he might have been a bit more cooperative. 'Your Dean's on an arm and a leg at Cas, get him to pay!' Alas, Dean and myself were so much adrift with the nightclub that we had nowhere to turn.

On March 2nd, I received a phone call from the brewery recoveries manager. 'David we don't want to bankrupt you, are you making progress selling the Railway, you're in court next Friday the 9th?'

'Well you could have fooled me.' I replied, 'In answer to your question the Railway sale has fallen through so what can we do in seven days?'

'I'll tell you what,' he stated, 'give us a charge behind the two banks at the Railway and we will work out a deal on the balance until it sells.'

'Why didn't you say that six months ago?' I barked, 'You'll have a deal by Tuesday March 6th.'

Well, my solicitor spoke to the brewery's solicitor to sort out the details and confirmed he would carry out the work necessary. I questioned him on timing and he categorically assured me it would be concluded by the deadline. 'Don't worry David, it'll be sorted.' were his final words on the subject and I therefore felt no need to attend the hearing fully expecting it would be withdrawn.

It had been difficult for me to accept the fact that Dean was also being threatened. The brewery knew he was only a sleeping partner having supported the business financially for many years and were fully aware that the buck stopped with me. However they had seemed determined to get their pound of flesh by including him in the petition based on a guarantee he had signed some four years prior. But hopefully that was now behind us, or so I thought. The following Tuesday - heartbreak!

'David?' my wife Mavis asked as I answered the phone in my office. 'Yes love, what is it?'

'I have just had a call for you from the Official Receiver, he wants you to ring him.' She then gave me his number.

It was 3 pm on Tuesday March 13th, very apt I remember thinking. I got through to the Official Receiver. 'What can I do for you?' I asked.

'Are you aware that you and your son Dean were made bankrupt last Friday in Wakefield County Court?'

My chest suddenly felt heavy, my stomach turned. 'But I was assured that the petitions were being withdrawn, everything was sorted, look, can I make a phone call and get back to you?'

I rang my solicitor, 'What the hell is going on?' I asked, 'You promised me last Tuesday afternoon that it was sorted, now I find that Dean and I are bankrupt!'

'Don't blame me!' he snapped raising his voice, 'I'm still waiting for their solicitor to send me a charge document!'

'Well I'll ring him now, myself.' I replied, 'I'll come back to you.'

I then rang the solicitor for the brewery, who had issued the petition.

'Well David that's rubbish, I'm still waiting for an answer to the fax I sent to your solicitor last Tuesday after I'd spoken to you, so don't blame us.'

I'll ring the brewery recoveries manager I thought, he must have had the last word, after all he was the decision maker in recoveries.

When I got through to him I asked, 'I thought we had sorted everything out, why have you gone through with the petition?'

'Well David, I just thought that you had walked away from it, your solicitor didn't comply so I allowed it to go through.'

I replied angrily, 'My solicitor is blaming yours and yours is blaming him, but you know I would never walk away, my son either, and not one of you had the decency to ring us, you're all a bloody disgrace!'

I hung up, the lousy rotten bastards, they sit on their fat arses in their ivory towers, take away two people's livelihoods which would have repercussions for a lot of other people too and not even bother to make a call. We could perhaps have attended court and pleaded our case, at least we would have gone down fighting. My mind was clouded, my heart racing from shock, anger and disbelief, I must do something, take a deep breath, think, maybe I can get it annulled, surely a verbal agreement should stand up? The Tuesday before I'd spent two hours agreeing the deal, all parties assuring me that they were happy with it, only to find that I have to accept such pathetic excuses from so-called professional people.

Well I certainly couldn't trust my solicitor but what about an insolvency specialist? I decided to contact one and see if the bankruptcy could be annulled.

Phone calls were made back and forth, and even when we had raised the money the Official Receiver blocked the move saying we were showing a preference to the Brewery. Well of course we were, we had already given them £6,000 of a £15,000 debt only to be told it had been gobbled up in costs and interest and they still wanted almost £15,000. And they talk about loan sharks. It will be interesting to see if the receivers claim the £6,000 back as preferential money paid, I doubt they will but they should.

After many more phone calls, the insolvency specialist informed me, 'Sorry David I can't get it annulled, you and Dean have been made bankrupt, I'm sorry, but it's not the end of the world you'll just have to start again.' I thanked him for his efforts and hung up the phone.

I called my son and broke the news, it's the hardest call I've ever had to make. My chest felt so heavy. I was mad at myself. 30 years I had sold beer for these people, 1971 to 2001 and for a few measly grand everything had come undone, the knock on effect would hurt others, that was inevitable, it really made me feel like a failure.

All my life I had been in the fast lane, then the last few months I was careering out of control, now my whole world was collapsing around me. I felt so helpless. I wanted to scream out, 'Please help me!'

It did not take long for me to realise everyone was looking at me, the Chinese whispers. I felt some were sorry, some glad, others indifferent and some just didn't believe it. But the people I care most about needed me and this is another path I now have to tread. I have to lead, head held high, proudly showing those closest to me that we are once again on the road to Shangri-la but this time we will drive a bit slower.

A couple of days after that disastrous Tuesday I had a brainstorm. Well I hope it was, only time will tell. I had stumbled on the telephone number of a contact in London, whom I had taken professional advice from previously regarding company and corporate recovery. I had not taken their advice or help which was folly on my part but just maybe they might be able to help. I rang them they were surprised to hear from me. It had been almost four years since we had spoken. They told me nothing could be done about the bankruptcies but confirmed all was not lost. They decided to explore the possibility of purchasing two pubs in Mavis', my wife's name. At least this compromise meant that we hadn't lost everything. I was encouraged and together with my family showing tremendous resolve plus with words of encouragement from friends and relatives I have begun to pick up the pieces.

Another brewery, Bass, have to date been tremendously supportive.

Postscript
The Miners Story

Crawling through the dark maze of narrow passages, following a shaft of light transmitted from his steel helmet, cramped and aching the miner struggled towards the distant face, thinking only of the reward at the end of his labours. He was leading a crocodile, whose tail was invisible except to the naked eye.

Overhead, high in the sky, amidst multitudes of stars, the pilots did their bit also for King and Country. The world was at war again.

The miners were allocated the task of keeping the home fires burning and this they did, every man jack of them knowing they would not be remembered in future years, but undaunted by this fact, they soldiered on. Their working world was perpetually black, absorbed through pores opened by the sweat of labour, sucked into lungs and forced down deep into their souls. A world inhabited by worms, by mice and men. Rats ran amok; too large to be contained in bottles, they were crushed by large steel capped, pit boots, then one felt free to eat. Not the rats, oh no, they were uninvited, unpalatable creatures.

Hacking and hewing manually to free the black nuggets, the miners worked on in silence, each man busy with his own private eye, patiently waiting for good hot nourishment when the shift was completed. Each to his own thought the majority of them. There was an exception however a man whose thought patterns stretched beyond to the future generation.

Instinctively he knew that the only impenetrable area was the mind's eye. Trade Unions would never answer the problems of mankind for they had already missed the boat. They could have formed and financed educational establishments, where working people's children could have had their inheritance presented on a silver platter, but the voices of the prejudiced were loud and vigorous in condemnation of this genius. Removing his helmet he rubbed across the hard material, wiping away the coal dust, spat on it and thought loudly. To hell with her. He knew there was no armour against fate that death lays its icy hand on Kings, but he longed only for warm hands to relieve his aching back. His wife had not travelled deeply enough, that was the truth. His mind moved forward. It ought to be compulsory for pontificators, criminals and the like to work off their angst on the coal black face of the underworld. They would know, first hand, the terrifying feeling of being trapped, walled in on all sides and how many then would survive in silence, using tools designed for today not tomorrow. He looked round, knowing that he would find no deputy standing in this area. They served their Masters in more congenial surroundings. None were queuing to work at this end of the tunnel, saving their prayer mats to use in roomier buildings, hollow statues to a vision existing only in spirit, inhabited by thin air. One began life as a miner, one ended life as a miner.

Trudging wearily along the road home he enjoyed the camaraderie of these fellows. Black men, one and all, they journeyed towards the Inn, where the landlady would have their pints of foaming ale, lining the bar. This would sleck the thirst, removing the dust from within, if not without. A cheering thought which helped overcome the first obstacle on the long journey home. Our miner was in the lead again, but his comrades arrived at the Inn before him, which was to his advantage today for as he neared his destination an old man appeared from out of the bushes and spoke to him. 'Take this,' he said and handed him an oval object placing it on the palm of the miners' hand. 'This is the seed of hope. Treasure it and your life will not have to be in vain.' Our miner was truly amazed and promised the 'gardener' that of all things he would indeed treasure this. Shaking hands the two men parted company each travelling a different pathway home.

Sorely perplexed, he continued as before, with the 'seed of hope' deep in the pocket of his working britches.

Later that week alone at the coalface, he mused over the words of the gardener, his mind in turmoil. Before him in that black hole he inhabited was a narrow shaft of light emanating from above. Perhaps a worm had crawled through the crust, but it shone a patch of earth in front of him. He knew this as the time and place to transfer his 'seed of hope' and digging his heel in the earth, he buried it there and then, watering it from his water bottle. Each day our miner travelled to his sacred shrine to water the earth. No one knew about this place except his wife, for they would have scoffed at his faith.

The war seemed interminable, night and day, the bombers flew over this tiny island devastating vast areas. Coal was produced daily throughout this terrible time.

Spring arrived at last and with it a momentous revelation for our miner. Visiting the secret shine, he saw that the first green shoots had broken through the earth. Each day thereafter, he made time to visit this special place, tending the young green shoots. Summer followed and a central bud appeared.

Autumn brought five smaller offshoots. His enthusiasm could be contained no longer and he crawled back to his workmates bidding them follow him. The miners were overwhelmed en masse by this revelation and news spread quickly throughout the village of this incredible phenomena. Of course, there were those who would not believe or were too frightened to actually travel the journey to see for themselves but it was a fact, there was no disputing it. The day the first flower bloomed was a day that will never be forgotten. It produced the only ebony rose he had ever seen and each shoot produced a rose of different hue.

The world was soon made aware of the rose and people travelled from miles around to see it. Photographs were taken. Members of the aristocracy travelled to see it. The King and Queen visited the mine. Gardeners from all corners of the globe were astounded and asked to purchase cuttings. It was not for sale. Women and men from other countries came to view it and our miner allowed cuttings to the chosen few.

To this day Sampson's Rose goes on growing, its roots firmly embedded deep in a Yorkshire coalmine. It flowers every year around Christmas time and every year the shades are different. This rose has never been reproduced in its original colours and form anywhere, although cuttings have flourished producing beautiful single roses. The miners named it Sampson's Rose.

Author Unknown